PLOT TWISTS AND RED HERRINGS:

A GUIDE TO MYSTERY GENRE TROPES

KIMBERLY WYLIE

CYPRESS CANYON PUBLISHING

To every writer out there with a story in their soul that must be told.

TABLE OF CONTENTS

Introduction

Writing a novel is a difficult process. Writing a novel that readers fall in love with, readers recommend to their friends, and one which actually sells is exponentially more so. Commercial success is a careful balance of unique creativity combined with knowing what readers in your genre want. For this reason, more and more authors are using a process referred to generically as 'writing to market.'

Writing to market involves crafting content that aligns with the interests, preferences, and demands of a specific target audience. It requires understanding the needs and desires of readers within a particular genre or niche and tailoring the content accordingly. This approach involves researching popular tropes, themes, and trends within the chosen market and incorporating them into the writing to enhance its appeal to the target audience. Writers who embrace the concept of writing to market prioritize delivering content that resonates with their readership, aiming to fulfill their expectations while also satisfying their own creative goals. By focusing on the market's preferences and expectations and combing that with well-developed characters readers connect with, interesting story arcs , and immersive settings, writers can increase the chances of their work being well-received, developing a fan base of readers eager to read the next book you write, and achieving commercial success.

This book was written to help you better understand the tropes your audience expects to find, in your genre. Think of it like having a grandmother who always makes a fresh batch of chocolate chip cookies for you when you arrive. You know, before you even walk in the door, her home is going to be filled with that rich aroma of butter and sugar, complemented with the irresistible undernote of warm, melty chocolate. You've been to her house so many times, and each time you are greeted with that wonderful scent. You'd be a little disappointed to walk in one time and find the home filled with the pungent fragrance of cabbage. Now, you might like cabbage. The cabbage may be absolutely delicious. But as you were driving over, then walking up the steps to grandma's house, your brain (and your tummy) was expecting chocolate chip cookies.

Readers come to a genre for those chocolate chip cookies. Even if you have the best cabbage recipe in the world, if your reader is hankering for cookies, they might be disappointed.

CHAPTER 1

What are Tropes?

Tropes are recurring themes, motifs, or storytelling conventions that are commonly used across various forms of literature, film, television, and other media. They serve as recognizable patterns or devices that audiences can easily identify and understand. Tropes often influence an audience's expectations and interpretations of a narrative. Tropes can encompass a wide range of elements, including character types, plot devices, settings, and narrative structures. While some tropes may be clichéd or overused, others can be effectively employed to enhance storytelling and evoke emotional responses from audiences.

In literature, tropes can be found in almost every genre and style of writing, from classic literature to contemporary bestsellers. For example, the "hero's journey" is a common trope in fantasy and adventure stories, featuring a protagonist who embarks on a quest, faces various challenges and adversaries, and ultimately achieves personal growth or triumph. Similarly, the "star-crossed lovers" trope is often seen in romance novels, where the romantic leads are kept apart by external forces or conflicts, adding tension and drama to the story.

In film and television, tropes are frequently used to create familiar narrative structures and character archetypes that strike a chord with audiences. For instance, the "buddy cop" trope pairs two unlikely partners—a by-the-book detective and a loose cannon—to solve crimes and catch criminals, leading to comedic and dramatic interactions between the characters. Likewise, the "final girl" trope is a common feature of horror movies, where a resilient and resourceful young woman survives encounters with a serial killer or supernatural threat, often becoming the sole survivor of the ordeal.

While tropes can sometimes be criticized for their predictability or lack of originality, skilled writers and creators can subvert or reinvent tropes to surprise and engage audiences in new ways. By playing with audience expectations and adding unexpected twists or variations to familiar tropes, storytellers can breathe fresh life into their narratives and offer unique perspectives on timeless themes and motifs. Ultimately, tropes are tools that writers and creators can use to craft compelling stories that connect with audiences on both intellectual and emotional levels. They sometimes become so popular they spawn entire genres centering on them.

Tropes are Useful for Writers

Tropes serve as fundamental building blocks for storytelling, providing writers with a shared language and framework to create engaging narratives. By drawing on familiar tropes, writers can quickly establish context, set expectations, and guide readers through the story. Tropes offer recognizable patterns and conventions that help structure plotlines, develop characters, and convey themes in a coherent and accessible manner. Additionally, tropes can act as narrative shortcuts, allowing writers to convey complex ideas or emotions efficiently and effectively.

Tropes develop over the history of a genre. In fact, even if you've never heard of the word 'trope' before and write a book in a genre you're well-read in, chances are you will naturally include at least one trope. Each book we read in a genre helps us, as authors, develop ideas about what we've personally enjoyed reading in stories, what we saw other authors use successfully, and (almost as importantly) what we've disliked and felt failed. It is one of the primary reasons to be reading everything you can get your hands on in your genre, from a wide variety of authors.

One of the key advantages of tropes is their ability to establish genre conventions and audience expectations. For example, the "chosen one" trope is a common feature of fantasy and adventure stories, signaling to readers the protagonist possesses special abilities or destinies that will play a crucial role in the plot. By incorporating this trope, writers can quickly immerse readers in a fantastical world filled with magic, adventure, and epic quests, tapping into the genre's core themes and motifs.

Furthermore, tropes provide writers with a rich source of inspiration and creativity. While tropes themselves may be familiar or even clichéd, it is the unique spin or interpretation that writers bring to them that makes their stories compelling and memorable. By reimagining or subverting familiar tropes, writers can inject freshness and originality into their narratives, offering audiences new perspectives and insights on timeless themes and motifs. This creative reinterpretation of tropes allows writers to innovate within established genres and push the boundaries of storytelling.

Tropes also facilitate communication between writers and audiences, creating a shared understanding and connection that transcends cultural and linguistic barriers. Through the use of familiar tropes, writers can tap into universal themes and emotions that have an impact on readers across different backgrounds and experiences. Tropes act as storytelling shorthand, enabling writers to set specific moods, stir certain reactions, and convey complex ideas with clarity and precision. This shared vocabulary of tropes fosters a sense of camaraderie and community among writers and readers, enriching the collective storytelling experience.

Moreover, tropes provide writers with valuable tools for character development and world-building. By incorporating archetypal character types and plot devices into their stories, writers can create compelling and relatable characters that strike feelings with audiences. Tropes such as the "reluctant hero" or the "wise mentor" offer writers a blueprint for crafting dynamic and multifaceted characters that undergo meaningful arcs and transformations over the course of the story. Similarly, tropes can help writers construct immersive and believable fictional worlds by providing familiar frameworks for cultures, societies, and environments.

In the end, tropes are invaluable tools for writers, offering a versatile and flexible framework for crafting compelling narratives. By drawing on familiar tropes, writers can establish genre conventions, inspire creativity, facilitate communication, and enhance character development and world-building. While tropes may sometimes be criticized for their predictability or lack of originality, it is the skillful execution and innovative interpretation of tropes that ultimately determine the success of a story. Through thoughtful and strategic use of tropes, writers can create stories that resonate with audiences on both intellectual and emotional levels, leaving a lasting impact on readers long after they have turned the final page.

Using Tropes Isn't a Cop Out

The use of tropes has been a subject of discussion amongst authors from every genre. Some feel that using tropes is a lazy, formulaic way of writing. This, they feel, leads to uninspiring and unoriginal stories that border on imitation.

I would argue this is completely false.

When used prudently, sparingly, and creatively, tropes will not only deliver on readers' expectations (resulting in happier and more engaged readers as they enjoy those chocolate chip cookies they are expecting) but also help you, the writer, in your story development. When used correctly, stories using the same trope can be completely different and equally successful.

Take, for example a comparison of J.R.R. Tolkien's protagonist, Frodo Baggins, in the *Lord of the Rings* series and J.K. Rowling's protagonist, Harry Potter, in the *Harry Potter* series. Both authors use the 'Chosen One' trope quite successfully. Both Harry and Frodo are average, every man characters chosen by fate to save the world. They both undertake and accomplish epic quests for the completion of their story. But these stories themselves are completely different tales, filled with a different cast of characters, in widely different settings.

Yes, using too many tropes can make your reading feel formulaic, predictable, even boring. Using tropes without the support of immersive settings, well-developed characters your readers will connect with, and an interesting and unique plot will cause your story to fall flat. But sprinkling them in artfully, and then caressing them in unique and exciting ways, with the support of great characters, settings, and plot, will help make your novel stand out in an ever-increasing tidal wave of published fiction. This is where your creativity transforms expected story elements and makes them masterful additions to your overall story.

CHAPTER 2

How to Use Tropes in Your Writing

There are three primary ways you can purposefully use tropes in your writing. These are: story development, editing, and marketing.

Using Tropes in Story Development

When developing ideas for your book, tropes can serve as valuable tools to inspire creativity and guide your storytelling. Start by identifying the genre or genres you're interested in exploring, as well as the specific tropes commonly associated with those genres. For example, if you're writing a mystery novel, you might consider incorporating tropes such as the amateur sleuth, the locked room mystery, or the red herring.

Once you have a basic understanding of the tropes within your chosen genre, use them as building blocks to construct your story. Consider how you can put a unique spin on familiar tropes or combine multiple tropes in innovative ways to create a fresh and engaging narrative. Experiment with different plot ideas, character archetypes, and setting concepts, using tropes as a framework to structure your brainstorming process. By leveraging tropes as a starting point for your creative exploration, you can harness their storytelling power to craft a compelling and original story that strikes a chord with readers.

Using Tropes During the Editing Process of Your Novel

You've birthed your story from your mind into reality. Hooray! But your baby isn't quite ready to enter the great, big world. You have now entered the incredibly important editing phase of book writing. When editing your manuscript, tropes can be valuable tools for assessing the effectiveness of your storytelling and identifying areas for improvement. Start by reviewing your manuscript with a critical eye, paying close attention to how you've incorporated tropes into your narrative. Evaluate whether you've effectively utilized tropes to enhance your plot, develop your characters, and establish the tone and atmosphere of your story. Look for opportunities to refine and strengthen your use of tropes, ensuring they contribute meaningfully to the overall cohesion and impact of your manuscript. If you use an editor or beta readers, ask them to read with tropes they expect to find in your genre in mind and how effectively (or ineffectively) they feel they have been used.

As you revise your manuscript, consider how you can subvert or deconstruct tropes to add depth and complexity to your storytelling. Challenge yourself to break away from predictable narrative conventions and explore new and unexpected directions for your plot, characters, and themes. Experiment with unconventional twists and interpretations of familiar tropes, pushing the boundaries of genre expectations while staying true to the essence of your story. By using tropes as a springboard for creative experimentation and innovation during the editing process, you can elevate the quality and originality of your manuscript, resulting in a more compelling and memorable reading experience for your audience.

Marketing Your Book with Tropes

When marketing your book, tropes can serve as powerful tools for attracting and engaging your target audience. Begin by identifying the key tropes that are prevalent in your book, such as those related to the genre, plot, characters, or setting. Use these tropes to craft compelling and resonant messaging that highlights the unique selling points of your story and appeals to readers who enjoy similar narratives. Leverage tropes to create attention-grabbing taglines, book descriptions, and marketing materials that effectively communicate the essence of your book and pique the curiosity of potential readers.

Additionally, consider how you can leverage tropes to establish connections with existing fan communities and niche markets within your genre. Engage with readers and influencers who are passionate about specific tropes or subgenres, and tailor your marketing efforts to align with their interests and preferences. Explore opportunities to participate in genre-specific events, book clubs, or online forums where discussions about tropes are common, and position your book as a must-read for fans of those tropes. By strategically leveraging tropes in your marketing strategy, you can effectively reach and ring true with your target audience, ultimately driving interest, engagement, and sales for your book.

CHAPTER 3

Categories of Tropes

As we've discussed, tropes, are foundational elements of storytelling. They offer writers a rich tapestry of tools to weave intricate narratives and engage audiences across various genres with expected storytelling elements. These narrative devices serve as essential building blocks that writers can manipulate and subvert to create unique and compelling stories. To better understand tropes and learn how to utilize them is by first understanding the five primary categories tropes fall into, each encompassing distinct aspects of storytelling. These four categories are: character tropes, setting tropes, genre tropes, and plot device tropes.

Mix and match tropes from a variety of categories to help you create a balanced story filled with not only story arcs your readers are hoping to read, but characters they love to meet, settings they are eager to explore, and more. Of course, you don't have to have a trope from every category. This is your creative license. But some sub-genres almost demand specific tropes. As an example, part of what makes a cozy mystery a cozy is the setting trope of Small Town Setting. Setting your cozy in a big city may not appeal to cozy lovers.

Now, let's take a look at the general categories of tropes.

Character Tropes

Character tropes encompass a wide array of archetypal personalities, traits, and roles that populate fictional worlds and drive narrative conflicts. From the noble hero to the cunning villain, character tropes provide readers with recognizable figures that navigate the complexities of the plot and engage with thematic elements. Remember, an expected character trope in your chosen genre is only as good as your development of that character. Be sure they are well-rounded beings your readers can emotionally connect with. Relying solely on the trope as your definition of the character will result in a character stereotype that readers won't enjoy.

Setting Tropes

Setting tropes encompass a diverse range of elements, including time periods, geographical locations, and cultural landscapes. These contribute to the overall mood and tone of the narrative. From sprawling metropolises to remote wildernesses, setting tropes prompt a sense of place that immerses readers in the story and enhances their emotional engagement.

Genre Tropes

Genre tropes are conventions, motifs, or themes that are characteristic of a particular genre or category of storytelling. These tropes serve to define and distinguish different genres from one another, providing audiences with expectations about the content, style, and themes of works within a given genre. Genre tropes can include recurring plot elements, character archetypes, setting conventions, and thematic motifs that are commonly associated with a specific genre. For example, the Detective Protagonist, red herrings, and plot twists are genre tropes commonly found in mystery novels, while the chosen one, epic battles, and magical creatures are genre tropes typical of fantasy stories.

Plot Device Tropes

Plot device tropes are narrative elements or techniques used by writers to advance the storyline, create tension, or resolve conflicts within a narrative. These tropes serve as essential tools in storytelling, shaping the trajectory of the plot and engaging the reader's interest. While some plot device tropes may be predictable or formulaic, skilled writers can subvert expectations and employ them in inventive ways to surprise and captivate their audience.

CHAPTER 4

The Mystery Genre

The mystery genre is a rich and diverse literary category that has captivated readers for centuries. At its core, mystery novels revolve around the investigation of a crime or puzzle, with the primary goal being to uncover the truth behind the mystery. Whether it's a murder, theft, or other criminal act, mysteries often involve a protagonist or group of characters working to solve the case, unraveling clues and piecing together evidence along the way. This genre is known for its suspenseful plots, intricate puzzles, and unexpected plot twists, keeping readers engaged and eager to uncover the truth alongside the characters.

One of the defining features of the mystery genre is its emphasis on suspense and tension. Authors skillfully build suspense by withholding key information, introducing red herrings, and creating a sense of uncertainty and anticipation as the story unfolds. This tension keeps readers guessing and invested in the outcome of the mystery, eagerly turning pages to uncover the truth. Whether it's a classic whodunit or a psychological thriller, mystery novels often play on readers' curiosity and desire to solve the puzzle, leading to a deeply immersive reading experience.

Another hallmark of the mystery genre is its wide range of subgenres and themes. From cozy mysteries set in quaint villages to hard-boiled detective stories in gritty urban landscapes, there is a mystery novel to suit every taste and preference. Some mysteries focus on the intricacies of forensic science and police procedure, while others delve into the complexities of human psychology and motive. Historical mysteries transport readers to different time periods, while legal thrillers explore the inner workings of the criminal justice system. This diversity within the genre guarantees there is always something new and exciting for mystery enthusiasts to discover.

Ultimately, the mystery genre offers readers more than just a thrilling whodunit; it also provides a window into the human condition. Through the lens of crime and investigation, mystery novels explore themes of morality, justice, and redemption. They delve into the complexities of human nature, shining a light on both the darkest impulses and the noblest virtues of humanity. Whether readers are drawn to the intellectual challenge of solving a puzzle or the emotional depth of exploring complex characters and themes, the mystery genre continues to captivate and inspire audiences around the world.

Mystery Sub-Genres

As mentioned, there are numerous sub-genres in the mystery genre. In fact, some of these sub-genres can blend a little at the edges. For this reason, some of the tropes we'll discuss are applicable to all of these sub-genres, and there are some that are commonly found in more than one. Of course, this doesn't mean you can't use a trope from a different sub-genre in your story, but don't forget the purpose of utilizing tropes is to give readers some story facets they expect to experience, so be sure to include those expected ones. To begin, it's important to know what sub-genre you're writing in, so let's talk about the ten most popular mystery sub-genres.

Amateur Sleuth (AS)

The amateur sleuth mystery genre revolves around ordinary individuals who find themselves embroiled in solving crimes, often against their will or out of curiosity. Unlike professional detectives or law enforcement officers, amateur sleuths typically have no formal training in crime-solving but possess keen observational skills, intuition, and a strong sense of justice. These protagonists come from various backgrounds and professions, ranging from cozy bakers and bookstore owners to retirees and hobbyists. The appeal of amateur sleuth mysteries lies in the relatable nature of the protagonists, as readers empathize with their struggles and root for them to uncover the truth. The genre often features cozy settings, quirky characters, and intricate puzzles, making it a favorite among mystery enthusiasts seeking engaging and light-hearted reads.

Examples of amateur sleuth novels:

1. *The No. 1 Ladies' Detective Agency* by Alexander McCall Smith
2. *The Sweetness at the Bottom of the Pie* by Alan Bradley
3. *Maisie Dobbs* by Jacqueline Winspear
4. *The Cat Who Could Read Backwards* by Lilian Jackson Braun
5. *The Unexpected Mrs. Pollifax* by Dorothy Gilman
6. *The Spellman Files* by Lisa Lutz

7. *Murder Is Binding* by Lorna Barrett

8. *One for the Money* by Janet Evanovich

9. *The Weed That Strings the Hangman's Bag* by Alan Bradley

10. *The Beekeeper's Apprentice* by Laurie R. King

Cozy Mystery (CM)

The cozy mystery genre, also known as the "cozy," is a subgenre of crime fiction that emphasizes a light-hearted and feel-good approach to storytelling. In cozy mysteries, the focus is less on graphic violence and gritty realism and more on creating a charming and cozy atmosphere for readers to enjoy. These novels typically feature amateur sleuths, often women, who find themselves caught up in solving crimes within their close-knit communities. Set in quaint villages, small towns, or picturesque countryside settings, cozy mysteries offer readers an escape to idyllic locales where they can immerse themselves in the intrigues of everyday life while unraveling a compelling mystery. With their engaging characters, witty dialogue, and satisfying resolutions, cozy mysteries provide readers with a delightful blend of suspense, humor, and heartwarming moments, making them a beloved and enduring genre within the realm of crime fiction. There are actually several sub-sub-genres in the cozy category, including: paranormal, culinary, animal, and others. It's important to note that although cozies typically feature an amateur sleuth, not all Amateur Sleuth sub-genre novels fall into the cozy sub-genre.

Some examples of cozy mysteries include:

1. *The Mysterious Affair at Styles* by Agatha Christie

2. *Murder on the Orient Express* by Agatha Christie

3. *A Murder Is Announced* by Agatha Christie

4. *Death on the Nile* by Agatha Christie

5. *The Cat Who Could Read Backwards* by Lilian Jackson Braun
6. *The No. 1 Ladies' Detective Agency* by Alexander McCall Smith
7. *The Sweetness at the Bottom of the Pie* by Alan Bradley
8. *Maisie Dobbs* by Jacqueline Winspear
9. *Death by Darjeeling* by Laura Childs
10. *Chocolate Chip Cookie Murder* by Joanne Fluke

Forensic Mystery (FM)

The forensic mystery sub-genre revolves around the use of forensic science techniques and evidence analysis to solve crimes. These stories typically feature protagonists who are forensic experts, such as medical examiners, crime scene investigators, or forensic pathologists, and they often work closely with law enforcement agencies to unravel complex cases. Forensic mysteries are known for their attention to detail and accuracy in depicting forensic procedures, making them popular among readers interested in the intersection of science and crime-solving. These narratives often involve intricate puzzles and meticulous detective work, as the protagonists use scientific methods to uncover clues, identify suspects, and ultimately bring perpetrators to justice. With their focus on scientific investigation and problem-solving, forensic mysteries provide readers with a captivating and intellectually stimulating reading experience.

Some examples of forensic mysteries include:

1. *The Bone Collector* by Jeffery Deaver
2. *Deja Dead* by Kathy Reichs
3. *Postmortem* by Patricia Cornwell
4. *The Silence of the Lambs* by Thomas Harris
5. *Blow Fly* by Patricia Cornwell

6. *The Body Farm* by Patricia Cornwell

7. *Trace* by Patricia Cornwell

8. *The Cold Moon* by Jeffery Deaver

9. *The Cutting Edge* by Jeffery Deaver

10. *Cross Bones* by Kathy Reichs

Gothic Mystery (GM)

Gothic mystery is a sub-genre of literature that combines elements of mystery and horror with a dark, atmospheric setting. Originating in the 18th century with classic works such as "The Castle of Otranto" by Horace Walpole, gothic mysteries often feature eerie and foreboding settings such as ancient castles, decrepit mansions, or isolated estates. The genre is characterized by its emphasis on suspense, supernatural elements, and psychological tension, as well as themes of death, decay, and the unknown. Protagonists in gothic mysteries typically find themselves entangled in sinister plots, haunted by ghosts, or confronting dark secrets from the past as they navigate the treacherous landscapes of these Gothic settings. Overall, gothic mystery offers readers a thrilling and immersive experience that combines elements of terror and intrigue in an atmospheric and haunting narrative.

Here are some examples of gothic mystery novels:

1. *Bloodless* by Douglas Preston & Lincoln Child

2. *What Ever Happened to Baby Jane* by Henry Farrell

3. *Rebecca* by Daphne du Maurier

4. *The Woman in the Mirror* by Rebecca James

5. *Wolf Winter* by Cecilia Ekbäck

6. *The Dark Room* by Jonathan Moore

7. *Inspector of the Dead* by David Morrell

Hard-Boiled Mystery (HBM)

The hard-boiled mystery genre is known for its gritty and cynical portrayal of crime and detection, featuring tough and street-smart private investigators as protagonists. Set against the backdrop of urban landscapes and seedy underbellies, these novels often explore themes of corruption, violence, and moral ambiguity. Hard-boiled mysteries are characterized by their fast-paced plots, sharp dialogue, and morally ambiguous characters who operate in shades of gray rather than black and white. The protagonists of these novels are typically loners who operate outside the confines of the law, navigating a world of danger and deception as they seek to uncover the truth behind complex and often sinister crimes. With a focus on realism and authenticity, hard-boiled mysteries offer readers a raw and unfiltered look at the darker side of human nature, challenging conventional notions of justice and morality in the process.

Some examples of hard-boiled mysteries include:

1. *The Big Sleep* by Raymond Chandler
2. *The Maltese Falcon* by Dashiell Hammett
3. *The Long Goodbye* by Raymond Chandler
4. *Farewell, My Lovely* by Raymond Chandler
5. *Red Harvest* by Dashiell Hammett
6. *Double Indemnity* by James M. Cain
7. *The High Window* by Raymond Chandler
8. *The Glass Key* by Dashiell Hammett
9. *The Black Echo* by Michael Connelly
10. *Devil in a Blue Dress* by Walter Mosley

Heist and Caper Mystery (HCM)

The heist and caper sub-genre of the mystery genre revolves around elaborate schemes, daring thefts, and intricate plots orchestrated by charismatic criminals or mastermind protagonists. In these stories, the focus is on the planning and execution of a high-stakes theft or robbery, often involving valuable treasures, priceless artifacts, or significant sums of money. The protagonists, typically a team of skilled individuals with unique talents and specialties, come together to pull off the perfect crime while navigating obstacles, outsmarting authorities, and evading capture. These narratives are characterized by clever twists, intricate schemes, and unexpected alliances, keeping readers enthralled as they root for the antiheroes to outwit their adversaries and emerge victorious.

Some examples of heist and caper mysteries include:

1. *The Hot Rock* by Donald E. Westlake
2. *The Hunter* by Richard Stark
3. *Beggars Can't be Choosers* by Bernie Rhodenbarr
4. *Get Shorty* by Elmore Leonard
5. *Crashed* by Timothy Hallinan
6. *The Good Thief's Guide to Amsterdam* by Chris Ewan
7. *Faking It* by Jennifer Crusie
8. *Flirting with Danger* by Suzanne Enoch
9. *The Heist* by Janet Evanovich and Lee Goldburg

Historical Mystery (HM)

The historical mystery genre blends elements of historical fiction with the suspense and intrigue of a traditional mystery. Set in the past, often during significant historical periods or events, these mysteries immerse readers in richly detailed settings and offer a glimpse into different eras. Typically, historical mysteries feature amateur detectives or professional investigators solving crimes against the backdrop of historical events, such as wars, revolutions, or cultural movements. The genre allows readers to explore different time periods while engaging in compelling whodunit plots filled with twists, turns, and red herrings. Through meticulous research and attention to historical accuracy, authors transport readers to another time, offering both entertainment and education.

Great examples of historical mysteries include:

1. *The Name of the Rose* by Umberto Eco
2. *The Alienist* by Caleb Carr
3. *The Historian* by Elizabeth Kostova
4. *The Shadow of the Wind* by Carlos Ruiz Zafón
5. *Mistress of the Art of Death* by Ariana Franklin
6. *The Thirteenth Tale* by Diane Setterfield
7. *Crocodile on the Sandbank* by Elizabeth Peters
8. *The Daughter of Time* by Josephine Tey
9. *Good Dog, Bad Dog* by Ki Longfellow
10. *An Instance of the Fingerpost* by Iain Pears

Legal Thriller (LT)

The legal thriller mystery genre combines elements of mystery, suspense, and courtroom drama, often featuring lawyers, prosecutors, and judges as central characters. These novels typically involve complex legal cases, high-stakes courtroom battles, and intricate investigations into crimes. Protagonists in legal thrillers are often attorneys or legal professionals who find themselves entangled in dangerous situations while seeking justice for their clients or uncovering the truth behind a crime. These stories delve into the intricacies of the legal system, exploring themes of morality, ethics, and the pursuit of truth. Legal thriller mysteries are known for their fast-paced plots, intense courtroom scenes, and unexpected twists, keeping readers completely engaged with the plot until the final verdict is reached.

Some examples of legal thriller mysteries include:

1. *When Next We Meet* by J.B. Millhollin
2. *The Mainwaring Affair* by Anna Maynard Barbour
3. *The #1 Lawyer* by James Patterson
4. *Last Dance* by Sheldon Siegel
5. *The Client List* by Robin James
6. *Final Justice* by Peter O'Mahoney
7. *The Exchange* by John Grisham
8. *Resurrection Walk* by Michael Connelly
9. *Double Jeopardy* by William Bernhardy

Noir Mystery (NM)

The noir mystery genre, characterized by its dark and gritty atmosphere, delves into the seedy underbelly of society, where moral ambiguity and cynicism reign supreme. These novels often feature hard-boiled detectives navigating treacherous streets, where corruption, betrayal, and violence lurk around every corner. Set against the backdrop of urban landscapes or smoky back alleys, the protagonists of noir mysteries are typically flawed antiheroes with a cynical worldview, navigating murky moral waters as they pursue justice or solve crimes. The atmosphere is often as crucial as the plot, with evocative descriptions creating a sense of foreboding and tension. Themes of existentialism, alienation, and disillusionment are common in noir mysteries, adding depth and complexity to the genre's exploration of the human condition in the face of darkness and despair.

Examples of noir mysteries include:

1. *Bloody January* by Alan Parks
2. *Every Shallow Cut* by Tom Piccirilli
3. *Firewall* by Henning Mankell
4. *A Gun for Sale* by Graham Greene
5. *A Long Time Dead* by Mickey Spillane & Max Allan Collins
6. *Bedelia* by Vera Caspary
7. *Angel Eyes* by Loren D. Estleman
8. *Blood on the Moon* by James Ellroy

Occult Mysteries (OM)

The occult mystery sub-genre of the mystery genre delves into the realm of the supernatural, blending elements of traditional mystery with occult themes, supernatural phenomena, and paranormal occurrences. In these stories, protagonists investigate crimes that are inexplicable by conventional means, often involving ghosts, demons, witches, or otherworldly forces. The settings may include haunted houses, ancient ruins, or isolated communities with dark secrets. As investigators delve deeper into the mysteries, they encounter occult rituals, forbidden knowledge, and arcane artifacts that challenge their beliefs and push the boundaries of reality. The atmosphere is typically eerie and atmospheric, with a sense of foreboding and dread permeating the narrative. Occult mysteries often explore themes of good versus evil, the power of belief, and the thin veil between the natural and supernatural worlds, captivating readers with their blend of suspense, intrigue, and supernatural intrigue.

While both the occult mystery and paranormal mystery sub-genres involve supernatural elements, they differ in their focus and approach.

The occult mystery sub-genre typically revolves around occult practices, ancient rituals, and mystical phenomena rooted in religious or mystical traditions. Characters may encounter witches, warlocks, or practitioners of dark magic, and the plot often centers on solving mysteries related to these occult practices or artifacts. Settings tend to include ancient ruins, secret societies, or secluded communities with ties to the occult. Occult mysteries often delve into themes of good versus evil, the power of belief, and the consequences of meddling with supernatural forces.

On the other hand, the paranormal mystery sub-genre explores a broader range of supernatural phenomena beyond occult practices. This may include ghosts, spirits, psychic abilities, extraterrestrial beings, or cryptids like Bigfoot or the Loch Ness Monster. Paranormal mysteries often involve characters investigating hauntings, poltergeists, or unexplained phenomena in contemporary or historical settings. While occult mysteries focus on specific occult traditions and practices, paranormal mysteries encompass a wider array of supernatural elements, allowing for more diverse storylines and settings. While both sub-genres incorporate supernatural elements, occult mysteries tend to focus on occult practices and ancient rituals, whereas paranormal mysteries explore a broader range of supernatural phenomena beyond traditional occultism.

Some examples of occult mysteries include:

1. *Opium and Absinthe* by Lydia Kang
2. *The Rules of Magic* by Alice Hoffman
3. *In the Shadow of Blackbirds* by Cat Winters
4. *The Golem and the Jinn* by Helene Wecker
5. *Affinity* by Sarah Waters

6. *The Club Dumas* by Arturo Perez-Reverte

Paranormal Mystery

Paranormal mystery is a sub-genre of literature that blends elements of mystery with the supernatural or paranormal. In paranormal mysteries, protagonists often investigate inexplicable occurrences, unexplained phenomena, or crimes involving supernatural elements such as ghosts, demons, or psychic abilities. These mysteries can take place in contemporary settings, historical periods, or alternate realities, but they all involve characters grappling with the unknown and confronting forces beyond the natural realm. Paranormal mysteries explore themes of belief, skepticism, and the boundaries between reality and the supernatural, offering readers a captivating blend of suspense, intrigue, and the uncanny. Whether delving into haunted houses, uncovering ancient curses, or solving crimes with the help of supernatural allies, paranormal mysteries provide readers with an exhilarating journey into the realm of the unexplained. Paranormal cozy mysteries are one of the currently most popular subsets of cozies, merging cozy mystery with paranormal mystery.

Examples of this include:

1. *None of This is True* by Lisa Jewell
2. *Shiver* by Lisa Jackson
3. *Undead Urges* by Amanda Lee
4. *The Other Side of the Road* by Andrea Bartz
5. *Hexcess Baggage* by Lily Harper Hart
6. *Three Tainted Teas* by Lynn Cahoon
7. *The Ghost Orchid* by Jonathan Kellerman
8. *Deadly Seeds* by Jenna St. James
9. *The Dead Letter Delivery* by C.J. Archer

10. *Chilled to the Crone* by Amanda Lee

Police Procedural (PP)

The police procedural mystery genre is characterized by its focus on the investigative procedures and methods employed by law enforcement professionals to solve crimes. These novels typically feature police detectives, forensic experts, and other law enforcement personnel as central characters who work together to unravel complex mysteries and bring perpetrators to justice. Set against the backdrop of urban landscapes or bustling cities, police procedural mysteries often delve into the intricacies of police work, including crime scene analysis, witness interviews, and the gathering of evidence. With meticulous attention to detail and a strong emphasis on realism, these novels offer readers a glimpse into the inner workings of law enforcement agencies and the challenges faced by those tasked with upholding the law. Combining elements of suspense, action, and procedural accuracy, police procedural mysteries provide readers with a compelling and immersive reading experience as they follow along with investigators on their quest for truth.

Examples of police procedural mysteries include:

1. *The Black Echo* by Michael Connelly
2. *The Bone Collector* by Jeffery Deaver
3. *Gorky Park* by Martin Cruz Smith
4. *Handy Man* by Helen Durrant
5. *Faceless Killers* by Kenning Mankell
6. *Rules of Prey* by John Sanford
7. *Knots and Crosses* by Ian Rankin
8. *The Surgeon* by Tess Gerritsen

Psychological Thriller (PT)

The psychological thriller genre delves into the depths of the human psyche, exploring themes of manipulation, paranoia, and psychological warfare. These novels often feature complex characters who grapple with their inner demons while navigating suspenseful and unpredictable plot twists. Unlike traditional thrillers that rely heavily on action and external conflict, psychological thrillers focus on the psychological and emotional turmoil experienced by the characters. Protagonists in psychological thrillers are often ordinary individuals thrust into extraordinary circumstances, facing off against cunning adversaries or grappling with their own inner turmoil. These stories are characterized by their tense atmosphere, unreliable narrators, and mind-bending plot twists that keep readers guessing until the very end. Psychological thriller novels challenge readers to question their perceptions of reality and delve into the darkest recesses of the human mind.

Some examples of great psychological thrillers include:

1. *Things We Do in the Dark* by Jennifer Hillier
2. *Gone Girl* by Gillian Flynn
3. *The Girl on the Train* by Paula Hawkins
4. *The Silent Patient* by Alex Michaelides
5. *Before I Go to Sleep* by S.J. Watson
6. *Shutter Island* by Dennis Lehane
7. *In the Woods* by Tana French
8. *The Talented Mr. Ripley* by Patricia Highsmith
9. *The Woman in the Window* by A.J. Finn
10. *Dark Places* by Gillian Flynn

Serial Killer Mystery (SKM)

The serial killer mystery sub-genre focuses on narratives centered around the pursuit and investigation of a serial killer by law enforcement or amateur sleuths. These stories often delve into the psyche of the killer, exploring their motivations, methods, and the psychological impact on both the victims and the investigators. Characters in serial killer mysteries may include detectives, forensic experts, and sometimes even the killer themselves, providing a multifaceted perspective on the unfolding events. This sub-genre is characterized by its dark and suspenseful tone, as well as its emphasis on the cat-and-mouse dynamic between the pursuers and the perpetrator. Overall, serial killer mysteries captivate readers with their chilling atmosphere, intricate plot twists, and intense psychological suspense.

Examples of serial killer mystery novels include:

1. *Long Dark Night* by Susan Lund
2. *Tagged by Death* by Judith A. Barrett
3. *One Last Step* by Sarah Sutton
4. *The Cold Call Killer* by Emmy Ellis
5. *Her Darkest Nightmare* by Brenda Novak
6. *The Killing Lessons* by Saul Black
7. *Avenging Adam* by Jodi Burnett
8. *Cold Blooded Liar* by Karen Rose
9. *Girl Without a Chance* by Rylie Dark

Suspense Thriller Mystery (STM)

The suspense thriller mystery genre is characterized by its intense and gripping narratives that keep readers on the gripped with suspense from start to finish. These novels often feature high-stakes situations, intricate plots, and fast-paced action, creating a sense of tension and anticipation that drives the story forward. The protagonists of suspense thrillers are typically ordinary individuals thrust into extraordinary circumstances, facing danger, betrayal, and moral dilemmas as they race against time to uncover the truth or thwart a sinister plot. Twisty plots, unexpected revelations, and pulse-pounding suspense are hallmarks of the genre, keeping readers guessing until the very end. With its adrenaline-fueled storytelling and heart-pounding suspense, the suspense thriller mystery genre offers readers a thrilling rollercoaster ride of twists, turns, and unexpected surprises.

Here are a few examples of suspense thriller mysteries:

1. *And Then There Were None* by Agatha Christie
2. *The Girl with the Dragon Tattoo by Stieg Larsson*
3. *The Da Vinci Code* by Dan Brown
4. *The Guest List* by Lucy Foley
5. *The Woman in Cabin 10* by Ruth Ware
6. *Angels and Demons* by Dan Brown
7. *The Turn of the Key* by Ruth Ware
8. *The 7 ½ Deaths of Evelyn Hardcastle* by Stuart Turton

Whodunit (W)

The whodunit genre, a staple of mystery fiction, revolves around a central question: who committed the crime? These novels typically feature intricate plots filled with clues, red herrings, and twists as readers follow along with the protagonist's investigation to uncover the identity of the perpetrator. The focus of whodunits is on the puzzle aspect of solving the crime, with readers encouraged to play detective alongside the protagonist, analyzing evidence and scrutinizing alibis to piece together the truth. The genre often culminates in a dramatic reveal, where the detective unmasks the culprit and exposes their motives and methods. Whodunits come in various subgenres, including cozy mysteries, police procedurals, and amateur sleuth mysteries, each offering unique twists on the classic mystery formula while keeping readers engaged in the thrill of solving the puzzle.

Examples of classic whodunit mysteries include:

1. *Murder on the Orient Express* by Agatha Christie
2. *Death on the Nile* by Agatha Christie
3. *The Thursday Murder Club* by Richard Osman
4. *Magpie Murders* by Anthony Horowitz
5. *One of Us is Lying* by Karen M. McManus
6. *The Cuckoo's Calling* by Robert Galbraith
7. *The Maid* by Nita Prose
8. *A Study in Scarlet* by Arthur Conan Doyle
9. *A Good Girl's Guide to Murder* by Holly Jackson
10. *Five Little Pigs* by Agatha Christie

Now that you have an idea of what sub-genre you'll be writing in, let's start looking at those tropes.

Following are the tropes most often found in the mystery genre. You'll find a brief description of each trope, followed by a notation of which sub-genres where you'll most often find that trope. You'll see this notated as the initials of each sub-genre. Of course, as noted earlier, there are no rules that say you can't use a trope from one sub-genre in a genre where it's not typically found. Just know there are tried and true tropes that readers are fond of seeing in each genre. We'll also discuss what readers love about this trope and what to watch out for with each.

Think about the last book you read. What tropes did you experience? Which did you enjoy? Where have you seen those tropes used before, and how did the author use them differently?

Really critically evaluating the books in your chosen genre will help you become a better writer.

CHAPTER 5

Character Tropes for the Mystery Genre

Character tropes can play a significant role in shaping your character's arc and development throughout your story. By incorporating familiar character archetypes into your narrative, you can establish a foundation that readers can easily recognize and relate to. However, it's essential to use character tropes thoughtfully and creatively to avoid falling into clichés or stereotypes. Instead, consider how you can subvert or challenge these tropes to create complex and multi-dimensional characters that defy expectations.

One way character tropes can impact your character's arc is by providing a starting point for their journey. For example, the "reluctant hero" trope often features a protagonist who initially resists the call to action but ultimately rises to the challenge. By introducing your character within this archetype, you can set the stage for their growth and transformation as they confront obstacles, face internal conflicts, and ultimately embrace their role as a hero. This trajectory allows for a compelling character arc that connects with readers as they witness the protagonist's evolution over the course of the story.

Additionally, character tropes can influence the relationships and dynamics between characters, further shaping their arcs and interactions. For instance, the "rivalry-turned-friendship" trope often features characters who start off as adversaries but gradually develop mutual respect and camaraderie. By incorporating this trope into your narrative, you can explore themes of loyalty, forgiveness, and redemption as characters navigate their evolving relationships. This dynamic adds depth and complexity to your characters' arcs, offering opportunities for growth, reconciliation, and meaningful character development.

Overall, character tropes can serve as valuable tools for crafting compelling and relatable characters, but it's essential to approach them with nuance and creativity. By leveraging character tropes effectively and subverting expectations when necessary, you can create richly layered characters with arcs that have an impact on readers on a profound level, enriching your story and elevating its impact.

Amateur Detective Trope (AS, CM, HM, PM, W)

Amateur Detective Trope Overview

The Amateur Detective trope is a common motif in mystery fiction, featuring protagonists who are not professional investigators but become embroiled in solving crimes out of personal curiosity, necessity, or a desire for justice. Unlike professional detectives, amateur sleuths often lack formal training or credentials but compensate with sharp intellect, intuition, and a knack for uncovering clues overlooked by law enforcement. From curious neighbors to amateur sleuths and amateur sleuths to amateur historians, these characters come from diverse backgrounds but share a common penchant for solving mysteries. Despite their amateur status, they frequently find themselves at the center of complex investigations, often proving their mettle by solving cases that elude even seasoned professionals. The Amateur Detective trope adds an element of relatability and accessibility to mystery narratives, allowing readers to immerse themselves in the investigative process alongside characters who are everyday people thrust into extraordinary circumstances.

The Amateur Detective trope is a popular element often found in various mystery sub-genres, adding intrigue and excitement to the narrative. One of the primary sub-genres where this trope frequently appears is the cozy mystery. In cozy mysteries, amateur sleuths, often portrayed as everyday individuals with no formal training in detection, find themselves embroiled in puzzling mysteries within their communities. These protagonists, driven by curiosity or a desire to help others, rely on their wits and intuition to solve crimes, bringing a unique charm and relatability to the genre.

The Amateur Detective trope is also prevalent in the traditional or classic whodunit mystery. In these novels, amateur sleuths often stumble upon crimes while going about their daily lives, whether it's through chance encounters or by being in the wrong place at the wrong time. These protagonists, typically ordinary citizens or amateur detectives, become entangled in complex mysteries and take it upon themselves to unravel the truth, often against the backdrop of a carefully constructed whodunit plot.

Additionally, the Amateur Detective trope frequently appears in the amateur sleuth mystery sub-genre. In these stories, the protagonist is thrust into the role of detective due to personal connections to the crime or a strong sense of justice. Amateur sleuths in this sub-genre may be retirees, hobbyists, or individuals with a vested interest in the case, such as family members of the victim or suspects. Their amateur status adds an element of unpredictability to the investigation, as they navigate unfamiliar territory and grapple with their own limitations while pursuing the truth.

Overall, the Amateur Detective trope is a versatile and enduring element that can be found across various mystery sub-genres, offering readers a diverse array of amateur sleuths and captivating narratives. Whether it's in cozy mysteries, traditional mysteries, or amateur sleuth mysteries, the

Amateur Detective trope brings a sense of relatability and authenticity to the genre, allowing readers to vicariously experience the thrill of solving crimes alongside everyday heroes.

Why Readers Love the Amateur Detective Trope

Readers are drawn to the Amateur Detective trope for several reasons, making it a beloved element in mystery literature. Firstly, amateur detectives often possess qualities that readers can relate to on a personal level. Unlike professional detectives who may seem distant or detached, amateur sleuths are typically ordinary individuals thrust into extraordinary circumstances. Their amateur status allows readers to empathize with their struggles and root for their success, creating a strong emotional connection between the reader and the protagonist.

Furthermore, amateur detectives bring a fresh perspective to the genre, offering unique insights and unconventional approaches to solving crimes. Unlike seasoned professionals who may rely on established methods and procedures, amateur sleuths often think outside the box, using creativity, intuition, and street smarts to crack the case. This element of unpredictability adds an exciting layer of suspense and intrigue to the narrative, keeping readers engaged and guessing until the very end. Additionally, amateur detectives often undergo personal growth and development throughout the course of their investigations, making their journey as compelling as the mystery itself.

What to Watch for When Using the Amateur Detective Trope

When incorporating the Amateur Detective trope into your novels, there are several facets you need to watch for. This includes:

1. **Establish Credibility:** Despite lacking professional training or credentials, the amateur detective should possess qualities that make their involvement in solving mysteries plausible. Develop their motivation, skills, or personal connection to the case to justify their role as an investigator.

2. **Avoid Unrealistic Competence:** While the amateur detective may possess natural intuition or curiosity, avoid portraying them as infallible or overly competent. Show their flaws, mistakes, and limitations to create a relatable and believable character.

3. **Provide Logical Reasons for Involvement:** Clearly establish why the amateur detective becomes involved in solving the mystery. Whether driven by personal stakes, a desire for justice, or sheer curiosity, their motivation should be compelling and logically linked to the plot.

4. **Respect Legal and Ethical Boundaries:** Acknowledge the legal and ethical implications of amateur detective work. Avoid glorifying illegal or unethical behavior, such as trespassing, tampering with evidence, or interfering with law enforcement investigations.

5. **Develop Realistic Consequences:** Explore the potential consequences of amateur detective work, both positive and

negative. Show how their actions impact the investigation, relationships, and their own safety. Convey the risks and challenges they face in pursuing the truth.

When using the Amateur Detective trope, strive for credibility, avoid unrealistic competence, provide logical reasons for involvement, respect legal and ethical boundaries, and develop realistic consequences. By adhering to these guidelines, you can create compelling amateur detective characters that enrich the mystery narrative and engage readers.

Examples of the Amateur Detective Trope

Embarking on a journey through the labyrinth of mystery fiction, one trope shines brightly as a beacon of amateur intrigue: the Amateur Detective. These intrepid individuals, often thrust into the heart of enigmatic circumstances by chance or curiosity, captivate readers with their unassuming yet relentless pursuit of truth. From curious civilians stumbling upon clues to retired professionals turning their keen minds to sleuthing, the Amateur Detective trope invites readers to join in their thrilling escapades. In this section, we delve into the world of amateur sleuths, exploring a diverse array of characters who defy convention and prove anyone, regardless of background or profession, can unravel the mysteries that lie hidden in the shadows. Here are some examples of novels featuring the Amateur Detective trope:

- In *The No. 1 Ladies' Detective Agency* by Alexander McCall Smith, Precious Ramotswe is the amateur detective protagonist in this series set in Botswana. She uses her intuition and keen observational skills to solve mysteries in her community.

- *The Cat Who...* series by Lilian Jackson Braun is a cozy mystery series that utilizes the Amateur Detective trope. In this series, Jim Qwilleran is a journalist. He adopts two Siamese cats who help him solve various mysteries that occur in the fictional town of Pickax, Moose County.

- The *Nancy Drew Mystery Stories* by Carolyn Keene is a classic example of an amateur detective. With her sharp intellect and bravery, she solves mysteries ranging from missing jewels to haunted houses.

- *The Sweetness at the Bottom of the Pie* by Alan Bradley also features the Amateur Detective trope. Flavia de Luce is an 11-year-old amateur chemist and detective. She solves murders in her small English village in the 1950s.

- In Umberto Eco's *The Name of the Rose*, Brother William of Baskerville is a Franciscan friar. He investigates a series of murders at a Benedictine monastery in medieval Italy. He displays amateur detective traits as he unravels the complex mystery.

These examples showcase the diversity of amateur detectives in literature, ranging from children to retirees, each bringing their unique skills and perspectives to solving mysteries.

Detective Duo Trope
(AS, CM, PM, PP)

Detective Duo Overview

The Detective Duo trope features a dynamic partnership between two investigators who work together to solve crimes. This duo often consists of contrasting personalities, with one member embodying traits like intuition, creativity, or unorthodox methods, while the other brings logic, analytical skills, or authority to the table. Their differing approaches complement each other, allowing them to tackle cases from multiple angles and overcome obstacles that one detective alone might struggle with. The dynamic between the duo is a key aspect of this trope, with banter, camaraderie, and occasional conflicts adding depth to their relationship. Whether they're a seasoned veteran paired with a rookie, two equals with different strengths, or even adversaries forced to collaborate, the Detective Duo trope provides ample opportunity for character development, witty dialogue, and engaging storytelling. Together, they navigate the complexities of the criminal underworld, unraveling mysteries and bringing perpetrators to justice while forging a bond that transcends the cases they investigate.

The Dynamic Duo trope is commonly found in various mystery sub-genres where teamwork and collaboration are essential components of solving crimes. One of the primary sub-genres where this trope is prevalent is the police procedural, where a pair of detectives or investigators form a close partnership to tackle complex cases. These duos often have contrasting personalities or skill sets, which creates dynamic interactions and enhances their ability to crack the case. Whether it's the seasoned detective paired with a rookie officer or two experienced investigators with complementary expertise, the Dynamic Duo trope adds depth and intrigue to police procedural mysteries.

Another mystery sub-genre where the Dynamic Duo trope thrives is the amateur sleuth mystery. In these stories, a pair of amateur detectives or crime-solving enthusiasts join forces to unravel mysteries in their community or pursue personal investigations. This dynamic partnership often involves friends, family members, or romantic partners who share a passion for solving puzzles and uncovering the truth. The amateur sleuth duo may bring different perspectives or specialized knowledge to the table, allowing them to pool their resources and work together effectively to solve crimes. Their collaboration not only drives the plot forward but also strengthens their bond as they navigate the challenges of amateur sleuthing.

The Dynamic Duo trope is also prevalent in cozy mysteries, where amateur sleuths team up with unlikely partners to solve crimes in small towns or quaint settings. These cozy duos often include a main character paired with a sidekick or quirky companion who assists them in their investigative endeavors. Whether it's a pet, a close friend, or a local resident with unique insights, the sidekick adds humor, warmth, and additional sleuthing skills to the mix, creating a dynamic and engaging partnership. Together, they navigate the charming yet perilous world of cozy mysteries, uncovering clues and confronting suspects while forging lasting friendships along the way.

Why Readers Love the Dynamic Duo Trope

Readers love the Dynamic Duo trope in mystery novels for a variety of reasons. First and foremost, the interplay between two distinct characters allows for rich character development and fascinating relationships. Whether it's the clash of personalities, the deepening of mutual respect, or the growth of friendship, the dynamics between the duo members add depth and complexity to the story. Readers enjoy witnessing the evolution of these relationships as the characters face challenges, overcome obstacles, and ultimately triumph together.

The Dynamic Duo trope often leads to engaging storytelling and compelling plotlines. The partnership between two characters with different strengths, weaknesses, and perspectives creates opportunities for collaboration, conflict, and unexpected twists. Readers are intrigued by the teamwork and synergy that emerge as the duo navigates the intricacies of solving mysteries, piecing together clues, and outsmarting adversaries. Additionally, the banter, camaraderie, and shared moments of triumph between the duo members provide moments of levity and emotional resonance amidst the suspenseful narrative.

Ultimately, the appeal of the Dynamic Duo trope lies in its ability to captivate readers with lively characters, intricate relationships, and riveting storytelling. Whether it's the classic pairing of detectives in a police procedural, the charming camaraderie of amateur sleuths in a cozy mystery, or the unexpected alliance between unlikely partners, the Dynamic Duo trope offers endless possibilities for immersive and entertaining mystery fiction.

What to Watch for When Using the Dynamic Duo Trope

Writing the Dynamic Duo trope can be a lot of fun, especially as the characters play off of one another. But there are some things to watch for. Here are some key considerations:

1. **Establish Clear Character Roles:** Define the strengths, weaknesses, and personalities of each duo member to create contrast and complementarity between them.

2. **Foster Organic Chemistry:** Develop authentic interactions and meaningful relationships between the duo members to enhance believability and reader engagement.

3. **Maintain Balance:** Make certain both characters contribute equally to the investigation or conflict resolution, avoiding one-sided dominance or dependence.

4. **Provide Character Growth:** Allow the duo members to evolve individually and within their partnership, facing challenges and learning from their experiences.

5. **Avoid Clichés:** As with all tropes, strive for originality and depth in character development and plot dynamics, steering clear of predictable scenarios and character traits.

6. **Incorporate Conflict:** Introduce tension, disagreements, or differing viewpoints between the duo members to add complexity and realism to their relationship.

7. **Utilize Teamwork:** Showcase the duo's collaborative efforts, problem-solving skills, and mutual support as they work together to achieve their goals.

The Dynamic Duo trope offers a compelling framework for creating engaging characters and dynamic narratives in mystery fiction. By paying attention to character dynamics, narrative balance, and storytelling nuances, you can effectively leverage this trope to captivate readers and enhance your storytelling prowess.

Examples of the Detective Duo Trope

In the realm of mystery literature, the Detective Duo trope stands as a testament to the power of collaboration and camaraderie in solving crimes. From the iconic partnership of Sherlock Holmes and Dr. John Watson to the modern-day investigative teams found in contemporary novels, the synergy between two sleuths brings a unique dynamic to the genre. This section explores some of the most notable examples of the Detective Duo trope, showcasing the diverse range of partnerships and the thrilling adventures they embark on together.

- *The Adventures of Sherlock Holmes* by Arthur Conan Doyle features Sherlock Holmes and Dr. John Watson—one of the most iconic detective duos in literature. Holmes, with his deductive reasoning skills, and Watson, with his practicality and loyalty, solve a variety of mysteries together.

- In Dashiell Hammet's *The Thin Man*, Nick and Nora Charles are a sophisticated and witty husband-and-wife detective duo who investigate a murder case in this classic mystery novel.

- *In the Woods* by Tana French features Detectives Rob Ryan and Cassie Maddox as partners in the Dublin Murder Squad. They investigate a murder case in a small Irish town, while navigating their complex personal and professional relationship.

- *The Body in the Library* by Agatha Christie stars Miss Marple, an elderly amateur detective, who often teams up with the police to solve crimes. In this novel, she collaborates with Inspector Slack to unravel the mystery of a woman's body found in the library of Colonel Bantry's home.

- *The Cuckoo's Calling* by Robert Galbraith (pseudonym for J.K. Rowling) has Cormoran Strike, a private investigator, and his assistant Robin Ellacott forming a detective duo as they delve into the suspicious death of a supermodel in London.

- In Stieg Larsson's *The Girl with the Dragon Tattoo*, Mikael Blomkvist, an investigative journalist, teams up with Lisbeth Salander, a skilled hacker, to solve a decades-old disappearance case involving a wealthy Swedish family.

These examples illustrate the dynamic partnerships between detectives in solving mysteries, showcasing the diversity of relationships and personalities that can form a successful detective duo.

Detective Protagonist Trope
(CM, FM, HBM, PP, SKM)

Detective Protagonist Trope Overview

The Detective Protagonist trope features a central character who serves as the primary investigator or sleuth in a story, often tasked with solving crimes or mysteries. These protagonists are typically skilled, intelligent, and resourceful individuals who possess keen observational skills, deductive reasoning, and a relentless determination to uncover the truth. Whether they are professional detectives, amateur sleuths, or private investigators, these characters are driven by a strong sense of justice and a commitment to seeking out the facts. Detective Protagonists often face personal and professional challenges as they navigate through complex investigations, confront dangerous adversaries, and grapple with moral dilemmas. Despite the obstacles they encounter, these protagonists are characterized by their unwavering resolve to pursue justice and bring closure to the cases they undertake. Through their compelling narratives, Detective Protagonists serve as both heroes and guides, leading readers or viewers through intricate plots filled with twists, turns, and revelations.

The Detective Protagonist trope is most commonly found in the sub-genres of police procedurals, hard-boiled mysteries, and cozy mysteries. In police procedurals, the Detective Protagonist typically works within a law enforcement agency, such as a police department or a special investigative unit, to solve crimes and bring perpetrators to justice. These stories often focus on the procedural aspects of police work, including crime scene investigation, interviews with witnesses and suspects, and collaboration with colleagues.

In hard-boiled mysteries, the Detective Protagonist is often a lone wolf or a private investigator who operates outside the bounds of traditional law enforcement. These stories are characterized by their gritty, noir-inspired settings and hard-edged protagonists who navigate a world of corruption, violence, and moral ambiguity. The Detective Protagonist in a hard-boiled mystery is typically driven by a strong sense of justice and a willingness to confront danger head-on in pursuit of the truth.

Why Readers Love the Detective Protagonist Trope

Readers often gravitate towards the Detective Protagonist trope because it offers them a compelling and relatable character to follow throughout the story. These protagonists are typically skilled investigators with a keen eye for detail, sharp deductive reasoning, and a strong sense of justice, which makes them captivating figures to root for. Additionally, the Detective Protagonist's profession often lends itself to exciting and suspenseful plotlines, as they navigate crime scenes, interrogate suspects, and piece together clues to solve complex mysteries.

The Detective Protagonist's role as a champion of justice appeals to readers' desire for closure and resolution in the face of wrongdoing. Whether they're working within a law enforcement agency or operating as a private investigator, these characters are motivated by a sense of duty to protect the innocent and hold wrongdoers accountable for their actions. This moral clarity provides a satisfying narrative arc for readers, as they witness the protagonist's journey towards uncovering the truth and delivering justice.

The Detective Protagonist's ability to outsmart criminals and solve seemingly impossible cases taps into readers' fascination with puzzles and mysteries. As the protagonist unravels the intricacies of the case, readers are invited to participate in the investigation, piecing together clues alongside the detective and attempting to uncover the truth before it's revealed in the story. This interactive element of the narrative can be highly engaging for readers, as they become invested in the outcome of the investigation and experience a sense of satisfaction when the mystery is finally solved.

Overall, the Detective Protagonist trope offers readers a captivating combination of compelling characters, suspenseful plotlines, and moral clarity, making it a perennial favorite in the mystery genre.

What to Watch for When Using the Detective Protagonist Trope

When using the Detective Protagonist trope in a novel, be mindful of several key factors to be sure the character remains engaging and the story compelling.

1. **Avoid Clichés:** While the detective protagonist archetype is well-established, try to avoid falling into clichés or stereotypes. Instead, focus on creating a nuanced and multi-dimensional character with unique traits, flaws, and motivations. Give your detective protagonist depth by exploring their personal backstory, struggles, and growth throughout the story.

2. **Balanced Competence:** While it's essential for a detective protagonist to be skilled at their job, they shouldn't be portrayed as infallible or all-knowing. Readers are more likely to connect with a character who faces challenges, makes mistakes, and learns from their experiences. Assure your detective protagonist encounters obstacles and setbacks along the way, which can add depth to their character arc.

3. **Character Development:** A compelling detective protagonist should undergo significant growth and development over the course of the story. Explore how their experiences and interactions with other characters shape their worldview, beliefs, and behavior. Allow your protagonist to confront their own flaws and limitations, leading to personal growth and self-discovery.

4. **Complex Relationships:** The relationships your detective protagonist forms with other characters can significantly impact the story's dynamics. Develop meaningful connections between your protagonist and supporting characters, such as partners, colleagues, suspects, and allies. Explore how these relationships evolve over time, adding depth and complexity to the narrative.

5. **Fresh Perspectives:** While the detective protagonist is typically the focal point of the story, consider incorporating diverse perspectives and voices to enrich the narrative. Introduce secondary characters with unique backgrounds, skills, and viewpoints that complement and challenge the protagonist's perspective. This can add richness and depth to the storytelling, offering readers a multifaceted view of the mystery at hand.

6. **Innovative Plotlines:** To keep the story fresh and engaging, strive to innovate within the detective genre. Experiment with

unconventional plotlines, twists, and settings that defy reader expectations and breathe new life into familiar tropes. Don't be afraid to take risks and push the boundaries of the genre while staying true to the core elements that make detective fiction compelling.

By paying attention to these aspects, you'll be able to effectively leverage the Detective Protagonist trope to create captivating mysteries that resonate with readers.

Examples of the Detective Protagonist Trope

In the realm of mystery literature, the Detective Protagonist trope stands as a cornerstone, captivating readers with its portrayal of skilled investigators delving into the depths of complex cases. These protagonists often possess sharp intellects, keen observational skills, and a relentless drive to uncover the truth. From iconic figures of classic detective fiction to modern interpretations, the Detective Protagonist trope has left an indelible mark on the genre, offering readers thrilling narratives filled with suspense, intrigue, and compelling characters. Let's explore a selection of novels that showcase the enduring appeal of this beloved trope. Here are some examples of the Detective Protagonist trope.

- Sherlock Holmes, in *The Adventures of Sherlock Holmes* by Arthur Conan Doyle, is the quintessential detective protagonist, known for his brilliant deductive reasoning and keen observational skills. Holmes, alongside his loyal companion Dr. John Watson, tackles a series of intriguing cases with unmatched precision and intellect, showcasing his ability to solve seemingly unsolvable mysteries.

- Hercule Poirot, in *Murder on the Orient Express* by Agatha Christie, is another iconic detective protagonist. In *Murder on the Orient Express*, Poirot finds himself aboard the luxurious train when a murder occurs, and he must use his meticulous attention to detail and astute psychological insights to uncover the truth behind the crime.

- Harry Bosch, in *The Black Echo* by Michael Connelly, is a tenacious Los Angeles police detective. Bosch is confronted with a complex case involving a body found in a drainage pipe, and he must navigate the gritty underbelly of the city to solve the mystery, demonstrating his dogged determination and unwavering commitment to seeking justice.

- Adrian Monk, in *Mr. Monk Goes to the Firehouse* by Lee Goldberg, is a brilliant yet eccentric former police detective turned private consultant with an obsessive-compulsive disorder. Monk investigates a deadly arson case involving a firefighter, employing his exceptional attention to detail and unique problem-solving methods to crack the case despite facing personal challenges.

- Sam Spade, in *The Maltese Falcon* by Dashiell Hammett, is a hard-boiled private detective. Spade becomes embroiled in a convoluted mystery surrounding the search for a valuable statuette, navigating a treacherous world of deception and betrayal in his quest for the truth, embodying the archetype of the tough, cynical detective protagonist.

Eccentric Detective Trope (AS, CM, HBM, PM, PP)

Eccentric Detective Trope Overview

The Eccentric Detective trope is a classic archetype frequently employed in mystery fiction, characterized by a detective or investigator who possesses unconventional methods, quirky behaviors, and idiosyncratic personality traits. Often portrayed as brilliant but eccentric individuals, these detectives eschew traditional investigative approaches in favor of their unique and sometimes eccentric methods of deduction. Whether it's Sherlock Holmes's remarkable powers of observation and deduction, Hercule Poirot's meticulous attention to detail and insistence on symmetry and order, or Adrian Monk's obsessive-compulsive tendencies and phobias, eccentric detectives often exhibit eccentricities that set them apart from their more conventional counterparts. Despite their peculiarities, these detectives are typically depicted as highly skilled and exceptionally perceptive, able to solve even the most perplexing of cases through their unconventional approaches and keen intellect. The Eccentric Detective trope adds depth and intrigue to mystery narratives, offering audiences compelling characters who bring a blend of brilliance, eccentricity, and charm to their investigations.

The Eccentric Detective trope is commonly found in various mystery sub-genres, adding a unique flavor to each narrative. In the cozy mystery sub-genre, the Eccentric Detective often takes center stage, providing a quirky and unconventional approach to solving crimes in small, intimate settings. These detectives may be amateur sleuths or professional investigators, but their eccentricities set them apart from the traditional detective archetype, offering a fresh perspective on the genre.

In the hard-boiled mystery sub-genre, the Eccentric Detective may appear as a secondary character or foil to the gritty protagonist. Their unconventional methods and idiosyncrasies contrast with the tough, no-nonsense demeanor of the main detective, creating dynamic interactions and adding depth to the story. Despite their eccentricities, these detectives are often highly skilled and resourceful, using their unique talents to crack tough cases and uncover hidden truths.

In the police procedural sub-genre, the Eccentric Detective may serve as a member of a larger investigative team, bringing their unconventional insights and unorthodox methods to the table. While their colleagues may initially dismiss or underestimate them, the Eccentric Detective often proves to be an invaluable asset, offering fresh perspectives and unconventional solutions to complex cases. Their eccentricities may clash with the strict protocols of police work, but their unorthodox approach ultimately leads to breakthroughs in the investigation.

Overall, the Eccentric Detective trope adds a layer of intrigue, humor, and unpredictability to mystery narratives across various sub-genres. Whether they're solving crimes in a quaint village, navigating the mean streets of a gritty urban landscape, or unraveling complex cases within a police department, these quirky characters bring a unique energy and charm to the genre, captivating readers with their unconventional methods and eccentric personalities.

Why Readers Love the Eccentric Detective Trope

Readers are drawn to the Eccentric Detective trope for several compelling reasons.These characters break away from the traditional mold of the stoic, by-the-book detective, offering a refreshing change of pace. Their eccentricities and quirks inject humor and levity into the narrative, providing moments of entertainment and amusement amidst the tension of solving crimes. This adds depth and dimension to the story, allowing readers to connect with the detective on a more personal level and making the investigative process more engaging and enjoyable.

Additionally, the Eccentric Detective often possesses a brilliant mind and unconventional approach to solving mysteries. Their unique methods and unorthodox thinking challenge readers to think outside the box and consider alternative solutions to the puzzles presented in the story. This can lead to unexpected plot twists and surprising revelations, keeping readers guessing and intrigued until the very end. Furthermore, the eccentricities of these detectives often serve as a mask for their deeper complexities and vulnerabilities, making them more relatable and sympathetic characters. Readers appreciate the depth and complexity of these individuals, as well as the opportunity to delve into their psyche and unravel the mysteries of their past. Overall, the Eccentric Detective trope offers a captivating blend of humor, intelligence, and humanity, making it a beloved favorite among mystery enthusiasts.

What to Watch for When Using the Eccentric Detective Trope

When incorporating the Eccentric Detective trope into a novel, be mindful of certain considerations to ensure its effective use. Here are some key points to watch for:

1. **Balance Eccentricity with Believability:** While eccentricities add charm to the character, they should not overshadow their investigative skills or credibility. Check the detective's quirks are plausible and consistent with their overall persona.

2. **Avoid Clichés:** While eccentric detectives are inherently quirky, steer clear of overused stereotypes or clichéd traits. Instead, strive to imbue the character with unique quirks and idiosyncrasies that set them apart from others in the genre.

3. **Develop a Compelling Backstory:** Delve into the detective's past to uncover the root causes of their eccentric behavior. A well-developed backstory can add depth and complexity to the character, making them more relatable and multidimensional.

4. **Use Eccentricity to Enhance the Plot:** The detective's eccentricities should serve a purpose beyond mere comic relief. Incorporate their unique traits into the investigation process, using them to uncover clues, solve puzzles, or outwit adversaries.

5. **Show Vulnerability Beneath the Surface:** While eccentric detectives may project an air of confidence, they should also exhibit vulnerability and flaws. Explore their inner struggles and insecurities, revealing layers of complexity beneath their quirky exterior.

The Eccentric Detective trope offers a wealth of creative possibilities, but it must be approached with care and consideration. By striking a balance between eccentricity and believability, avoiding clichés, developing a compelling backstory, using eccentricity to enhance the plot, and showing vulnerability beneath the surface, you can effectively utilize this trope to craft memorable and engaging characters in your mystery novels.

Examples of the Eccentric Detective Trope

Within the vast landscape of mystery literature, the Eccentric Detective trope adds a unique flavor, injecting quirks, eccentricities, and unconventional methods into investigative narratives. These characters often defy conventional norms, captivating readers with their idiosyncrasies and unorthodox approaches to solving mysteries. Let's delve into a selection of novels where the Eccentric Detective takes center stage, bringing their eccentricities to the forefront of thrilling investigations.

- In Arthur Conan Doyle's *The Adventures of Sherlock Holmes* we find the quintessential example of the Eccentric Detective trope, Sherlock Holmes is renowned for his brilliant deductive reasoning, remarkable attention to detail, and eccentric behavior. His unconventional methods, such as playing the violin at odd hours or conducting experiments in his apartment at 221B Baker Street, set him apart from traditional investigators. In each story, Holmes's eccentricities complement his unparalleled intellect, making him an enduring icon of detective fiction.

- Dirk Gently, the titular character of Douglas Adam' *Dirk Gently's Holistic Detective Agency*, is a holistic detective who believes in the interconnectedness of all things. His eccentric methods, which involve following hunches and trusting in the fundamental interconnectedness of the universe, often lead to unconventional solutions. Gently's eccentricities, including his tendency to rely on "the fundamental interconnectedness of all things" rather than traditional investigative techniques, make him a memorable addition to the world of detective fiction.

- In *Moon Over Soho* by Ben Aaronovitch, Detective Inspector Peter Grant discovers he has a talent for magic and joins a special branch of the London Metropolitan Police dedicated to investigating supernatural crimes. Grant's unconventional background, coupled with his dry wit and unorthodox methods, make him a memorable addition to the genre. As he navigates the complexities of magical London, Grant's eccentricities and unique perspective set him apart from traditional detectives.

The Eccentric Detective trope adds depth, humor, and intrigue to mystery novels, offering readers a refreshing departure from traditional investigative archetypes. Through their idiosyncrasies, unorthodox methods, and unconventional approaches to solving mysteries, these characters challenge readers' expectations and keep them engaged from the first page to the last. Whether they're playing the violin in Baker Street or unraveling the interconnectedness of the universe, Eccentric Detectives continue to captivate audiences with their eccentricities and unparalleled brilliance.

Femme Fatale Trope
(GM, HCM, LT, NM, PT)

Femme Fatale Overview

The Femme Fatale trope is a character archetype commonly found in mystery, thriller, and noir genres, characterized by a seductive and manipulative woman who uses her charm and allure to ensnare and manipulate male protagonists. Often depicted as mysterious and enigmatic, the Femme Fatale is skilled in the art of deception and manipulation, using her sexuality and wit to achieve her own ends, which may include luring unsuspecting victims into dangerous situations or orchestrating elaborate schemes for personal gain. The Femme Fatale is typically portrayed as morally ambiguous, blurring the lines between protagonist and antagonist, and posing a formidable challenge to the male protagonist's moral compass and sense of control. Despite her allure, the Femme Fatale is often depicted as a tragic figure, ultimately meeting a tragic end or facing the consequences of her actions. This trope reflects cultural anxieties surrounding female sexuality and power, presenting a complex and compelling portrayal of female agency and autonomy within the confines of a patriarchal society.

The Femme Fatale trope is most commonly found in mystery sub-genres that feature elements of noir fiction, legal thrillers, and psychological thrillers. These sub-genres often emphasize complex characters, moral ambiguity, and intricate plots, making them fertile ground for the inclusion of a Femme Fatale character. Noir mystery is characterized by its gritty, cynical portrayal of urban life, morally ambiguous characters, and hard-boiled detectives. Femme Fatale characters often play a central role in these stories, using their seductive charms and manipulative tactics to ensnare protagonists in dangerous situations.

In contrast, psychological thrillers delve into the inner workings of the human mind, exploring themes of deception, manipulation, and psychological manipulation. Femme Fatale characters may use their psychological prowess to manipulate and control others This often leads protagonists down dark and twisted paths as they unravel the mysteries at hand. Lastly, legal thrillers center around courtroom drama, legal proceedings, and the pursuit of justice. Femme Fatale characters may appear as witnesses, defendants, or antagonists, using their allure and cunning to manipulate legal outcomes and influence the course of justice.

In these mystery sub-genres, Femme Fatale characters are often portrayed as seductive, enigmatic, and morally ambiguous figures who blur the lines between ally and adversary. Their presence adds an element of danger, intrigue, and unpredictability to the narrative, keeping readers engaged as they navigate the twists and turns of the mystery.

Why Readers Love the Femme Fatale Trope

Readers are drawn to the Femme Fatale trope for several reasons. This character trope adds complexity, intrigue, and suspense to a story. Femme Fatale characters exude an aura of mystery and allure that captivates readers. Their enigmatic personalities and hidden agendas create a sense of anticipation and curiosity, compelling readers to unravel the secrets behind their actions.

Femme Fatales possess a dangerous charm that is both alluring and unsettling. Their seductive appeal and manipulative tactics draw protagonists—and readers—into a web of intrigue and suspense, heightening the tension and suspense of the narrative. The presence of a Femme Fatale injects conflict and drama into the narrative, driving the plot forward and keeping readers engaged. Their manipulation of other characters and involvement in clandestine activities create a sense of urgency and unpredictability that propels the story toward its climax.

Despite their often-villainous roles, Femme Fatales are portrayed as strong, independent women who wield power and agency in a male-dominated world. Readers are drawn to their defiance of societal norms and expectations, finding inspiration in their ability to control their own destinies, even if it comes at a cost. Overall, the Femme Fatale trope appeals to readers because it embodies themes of mystery, danger, and empowerment, offering a compelling and multifaceted character archetype that adds depth and intrigue to mystery stories.

What to Watch for When Using the Femme Fatale Trope

When using the Femme Fatale trope in a novel, be mindful of several key considerations to guarnatee its effective and nuanced portrayal:

1. **Avoid Stereotypes**: While Femme Fatales are often portrayed as seductive and manipulative, strive to avoid falling into clichés and

stereotypes. Instead, focus on developing multidimensional characters with depth and complexity.

2. **Provide Backstory:** To humanize the Femme Fatale and add depth to her character, provide backstory that explains her motivations and actions. Explore her past experiences, traumas, and relationships to shed light on her behavior.

3. **Avoid Objectification:** While Femme Fatales are often depicted as alluring and sexually confident, avoid reducing them to mere objects of desire. Ascertain their sexuality is portrayed in a respectful and empowering manner, rather than as a means of exploitation.

4. **Subvert Expectations:** To keep the trope fresh and engaging, consider subverting audience expectations by giving the Femme Fatale unexpected traits or motivations. Challenge stereotypes and explore new angles to keep readers guessing.

5. **Develop Other Characters:** While the Femme Fatale is a central figure in the narrative, it's important to develop other characters in the story as well. Give depth to protagonists, antagonists, and supporting characters to create a rich and immersive world.

6. **Explore Themes:** Use the Femme Fatale trope as an opportunity to explore themes such as power, agency, and gender dynamics. Delve into complex moral dilemmas and ethical questions raised by her actions, adding depth and resonance to the narrative.

7. **Provide Resolution:** In the resolution of the story, be certain the Femme Fatale's character arc is brought to a satisfying conclusion.

Whether she experiences redemption, punishment, or ambiguity, provide closure that feels earned and thematically resonant.

By approaching the Femme Fatale trope with nuance, depth, and creativity, you can create compelling characters and narratives that captivate readers. By avoiding stereotypes, providing backstory, and subverting expectations, you can breathe new life into this classic trope, exploring complex themes and delivering satisfying resolutions. With careful consideration and thoughtful execution, the Femme Fatale trope can add intrigue, suspense, and depth to mystery novels, enriching the storytelling experience for readers.

Examples of the Femme Fatale Trope

The Femme Fatale trope has long been a staple of mystery literature, introducing enigmatic and seductive female characters who often lead protagonists into dangerous and morally ambiguous situations. These characters wield their charm and allure as weapons, manipulating those around them to achieve their own ends. Following are a selection of novels where the Femme Fatale takes center stage, enthralling readers with her irresistible allure and mysterious intentions.

- Brigid O'Shaughnessy, also known as Miss Wonderly, in Dashiell Hammett's *The Maltese Falcon,* epitomizes the Femme Fatale archetype in this classic detective novel. Her seductive charm and manipulative nature draw private investigator Sam Spade into a web of intrigue and deceit as they become embroiled in the hunt for a valuable statuette. O'Shaughnessy's complex motives and willingness to use her allure to achieve her goals make her a quintessential Femme Fatale.

- In *Gone Girl* by Gillian Flynn, Amy Dunne emerges as a modern-day Femme Fatale in this gripping psychological thriller. As the novel unfolds, Amy's carefully crafted facade of the perfect wife begins to unravel, revealing a calculating and manipulative nature beneath. Through her cunning manipulation of those around her, Amy ensnares both the protagonist, Nick Dunne, and the reader in a twisted game of cat and mouse.

- In Raymon Chandler's *The Big Sleep*, Vivian Sternwood Rutledge, one of the central characters in this classic noir novel, fits the Femme Fatale archetype perfectly. Her seductive charm and ambiguous motives draw private detective Philip Marlowe into a labyrinthine plot involving blackmail, murder, and betrayal. Vivian's allure and manipulative nature keep Marlowe—and readers—guessing until the very end.

- Phyllis Dietrichson is the quintessential Femme Fatale in *Double Indemnity* by James Cain. She lures insurance salesman Walter Huff into a scheme to murder her husband for the insurance money. Phyllis's seductive charm and manipulative tactics drive the plot forward, leading to a series of twists and betrayals. Her calculated actions and willingness to use her allure as a weapon make her a classic example of the Femme Fatale archetype.

The Femme Fatale trope continues to captivate readers with its portrayal of complex and enigmatic female characters who wield their allure as a powerful weapon. These characters enthrall readers with their mysterious motives, manipulative tactics, and seductive charm. Femme Fatales leave an indelible mark on the world of mystery literature, reminding us danger often comes in the most alluring of packages.

Hard-Boiled Detective Trope (FM, HBM, NM, SKM)

Hard-Boiled Detective Trope Overview

The Hard-Boiled Detective trope is a hallmark of mystery and crime fiction, characterized by tough, cynical, and morally ambiguous private investigators navigating the gritty underbelly of society to crack cases. These detectives often operate outside the confines of the law, employing unorthodox methods and a no-nonsense attitude to get results. Their world is one of seedy bars, back alleys, and shadowy figures, where violence and corruption lurk around every corner. Hard-boiled detectives are typically haunted by their own troubled pasts and inner demons, which fuel their relentless pursuit of justice, often at great personal cost. The narrative style of hard-boiled detective stories is marked by terse dialogue, vivid descriptions of urban landscapes, and a sense of existential disillusionment with the world. Despite their hardened exteriors, these detectives often possess a strong moral compass, driven by a deep-seated desire to see justice served, even in a world where the lines between right and wrong are blurred.

The Hard-Boiled Detective trope is a staple of the hard-boiled mystery sub-genre, known for its gritty, noir-inspired narratives featuring tough and cynical protagonists. This trope is often found in detective fiction set in urban environments, where crime and corruption abound. Hard-boiled detectives typically operate outside the constraints of the law, navigating a morally ambiguous world where justice is often elusive.

One of the most common settings for stories featuring the Hard-Boiled Detective trope is the mean streets of a bustling metropolis, such as Los Angeles, New York City, or Chicago. These urban landscapes serve as fertile ground for gritty tales of crime and intrigue, where the detective must navigate through a labyrinth of alleyways, seedy bars, and back alleys to uncover the truth.

The Hard-Boiled Detective trope is frequently employed in the noir mystery sub-genre, characterized by their dark and atmospheric tone, morally ambiguous characters, and intricate plots. These narratives often delve into themes of corruption, betrayal, and existential despair, reflecting the bleak realities of urban life. Hard-boiled detectives are typically depicted as loners, haunted by their past and driven by a relentless pursuit of justice, even as they grapple with their own inner demons.

The Hard-Boiled Detective trope is a quintessential element of hard-boiled mystery fiction, offering readers a glimpse into the gritty underbelly of urban life and the complex psyche of its flawed protagonists. Whether navigating through the mean streets of a crime-ridden city or confronting the shadows of their own past, hard-boiled detectives captivate readers with their gritty realism and unwavering determination to seek truth and justice in a world fraught with darkness and deceit.

Readers are drawn to the Hard-Boiled Detective trope for its gritty realism and morally complex characters. These detectives are often portrayed as flawed individuals who operate in a world where the line between right and wrong is blurred. Their cynical outlook and tough exterior make them compelling protagonists, as readers are intrigued by their ability to navigate the murky waters of crime and corruption.

Additionally, the Hard-Boiled Detective trope offers readers a glimpse into the darker aspects of society, where justice is not always served and moral ambiguity reigns supreme. This exploration of the human condition, with its flaws and complexities, strike a chord with readers who are drawn to stories that delve into the complexities of human nature. Moreover, the gritty and atmospheric settings often associated with hard-boiled detective fiction, such as smoky bars, dimly lit alleys, and rain-soaked streets, add to the immersive experience and captivate readers with their vivid imagery and evocative storytelling.

In essence, readers love the Hard-Boiled Detective trope because it provides them with gripping narratives, complex characters, and thought-provoking themes. Whether it's unraveling a tangled web of deceit or confronting their own inner demons, hard-boiled detectives captivate readers with their unyielding determination and relentless pursuit of truth in a world fraught with danger and deception.

What to Watch for When Using the Hard-Boiled Detective Trope

When incorporating the Hard-Boiled Detective trope into your novel, it's essential to strike a balance between authenticity and cliché. While this archetype offers plenty of opportunities for compelling storytelling, there are certain pitfalls to avoid to be certain your narrative remains fresh and engaging.

1. **Avoid Stereotypes:** While hard-boiled detectives are often portrayed as tough, cynical, and morally ambiguous, be careful not to rely too heavily on stereotypes. Give your character depth and complexity by exploring their motivations, vulnerabilities, and moral compass.

2. **Develop Unique Characteristics:** To distinguish your hard-boiled detective from others in the genre, give them distinctive traits, quirks, or backstory. Whether it's a unique skill, a troubled past, or a personal code of ethics, these details can make your character more memorable and relatable to readers.

3. **Avoid Excessive Grittiness:** While gritty settings and tough dialogue are hallmarks of hard-boiled detective fiction, be mindful not to overdo it. Too much grimness can overshadow other aspects of your story, such as plot development and character relationships. Balance gritty realism with moments of levity or introspection to keep your narrative engaging.

4. **Subvert Expectations:** To keep your story fresh and unpredictable, consider subverting common tropes associated with the hard-boiled detective genre. Challenge reader

expectations by introducing unexpected plot twists, moral dilemmas, or unconventional characters that defy stereotypes.

5. **Emphasize Character Growth:** While hard-boiled detectives are often depicted as jaded loners, don't overlook opportunities for character growth and development. Allow your protagonist to evolve over the course of the story, confronting their flaws, facing personal challenges, and ultimately, finding redemption or resolution.

By being mindful of these items, you can effectively utilize the Hard-Boiled Detective trope in your novel while avoiding clichés and creating a compelling and original narrative that rings true with readers.

Examples of the Hard-Boiled Detective Trope

The Hard-Boiled Detective trope has long been a hallmark of mystery fiction, introducing gritty, tough-as-nails investigators who navigate the seedy underbelly of crime with unflinching resolve. These protagonists often find themselves embroiled in complex cases filled with danger, violence, and moral ambiguity, relying on their street smarts and no-nonsense attitude to crack the toughest of cases. Following are some examples of this hard-hitting trope in action.

- Philip Marlowe, in *The Big Sleep* by Raymond Chandler, the iconic private investigator, epitomizes the Hard-Boiled Detective archetype in this classic noir novel. With his sharp wit, tough demeanor, and penchant for hard liquor, Marlowe navigates the seedy streets of Los Angeles as he delves into a convoluted case involving blackmail, murder, and betrayal. His unyielding determination to uncover the truth, even in the face of danger, showcases his quintessential Hard-Boiled nature.

- In *The Maltese Falcon* by Dashiell Hammett, Sam Spade is the no-nonsense detective at the heart of this iconic novel. He embodies the Hard-Boiled Detective trope with his pragmatic approach to solving crimes. As he becomes embroiled in the hunt for a valuable statuette, Spade navigates a treacherous web of deceit and double-crosses with steely resolve. His unapologetic demeanor, penchant for violence when necessary, and commitment to his own moral code make him a archetypal Hard-Boiled protagonist.

- In *The Maltese Vulture* by D. B. Borton, private investigator Bartholomew Beck is thrust into a world of intrigue and danger when he's hired to find a missing woman. Beck's gritty demeanor, dry wit, and willingness to bend the rules make him a classic example of the Hard-Boiled Detective trope. As he navigates the seedy underbelly of his city, Beck confronts corruption, betrayal, and violence with unwavering determination.

The Hard-Boiled Detective trope continues to captivate readers with its portrayal of gritty, no-nonsense investigators who navigate the dangerous world of crime with unflinching resolve. From classic noir novels to modern thrillers, these protagonists captivate readers with their sharp wit, unyielding determination, and uncompromising pursuit of justice. Whether they're confronting corruption, violence, or moral ambiguity, Hard-Boiled Detectives leave an indelible mark on the world of mystery literature, reminding us sometimes, the toughest cases require the toughest investigators.

Private Investigator Trope
(HBM, NM, W)

Private Investigator Trope Overview

The Private Investigator trope is a classic archetype in mystery fiction, featuring protagonists who work independently as hired detectives to solve cases on behalf of clients. These characters often operate outside the constraints of law enforcement, allowing them greater freedom to pursue leads and uncover secrets without the bureaucratic red tape. Private investigators are typically depicted as resourceful, street-smart individuals with a keen eye for detail and a knack for navigating the seedy underbelly of society. From hard-boiled gumshoes to suave and sophisticated operatives, private investigators come in various forms but share a common commitment to uncovering the truth. Their cases range from routine background checks to complex murder mysteries, and their methods may include surveillance, interrogation, and undercover work. The Private Investigator trope adds an element of intrigue and suspense to mystery narratives, as these lone wolves navigate danger and deception in pursuit of justice.

The Private Investigator trope is a staple in various mystery sub-genres, adding depth and intrigue to the narrative. This versatile character archetype is commonly featured in hard-boiled mysteries, where they navigate gritty urban landscapes and confront criminal underworlds. In these stories, the private investigator often operates outside the constraints of law enforcement, using their street smarts and resourcefulness to crack tough cases. Their morally ambiguous nature and willingness to bend the rules make them compelling protagonists in tales of corruption, betrayal, and redemption.

The Private Investigator trope is also prevalent in noir mysteries, a sub-genre characterized by its dark and cynical tone. Set against the backdrop of seedy city streets and shadowy alleys, these stories delve into the murky depths of human nature, where morality is often obscured by shades of gray. Private investigators in noir fiction are typically flawed antiheroes grappling with their own demons while navigating treacherous investigations filled with deceit and double-crosses. Their moral ambiguity and existential struggles mirror the morally complex world they inhabit, adding layers of complexity to the narrative.

The Private Investigator trope finds a home in the whodunit sub-genre. In traditional detective stories, private investigators serve as lone wolves or partners working independently of law enforcement agencies. Whether tackling murder mysteries, missing persons cases, or corporate espionage, these protagonists employ deductive reasoning, keen observation skills, and a dogged determination to uncover the truth. Their relentless pursuit of justice, coupled with their knack for solving puzzles, makes them beloved figures in the realm of mystery literature.

Why Readers Love the Private Investigator Trope

Readers are drawn to the Private Investigator trope for its intriguing blend of characteristics that make for compelling storytelling. Private investigators often embody the archetype of the lone wolf, a figure who operates on the fringes of society and is unafraid to challenge authority. This independence and rugged individualism connect with readers who admire characters who chart their own course and defy conventions. Additionally, private investigators are often portrayed as underdogs, taking on cases others have overlooked or dismissed. Their determination to seek justice for the marginalized and forgotten taps into readers' sense of empathy and justice, making them root for these protagonists.

The private investigator's role as a truth-seeker appeals to readers' curiosity and desire for resolution. Whether it's solving a murder, uncovering a conspiracy, or unraveling a web of lies, these characters embark on journeys of discovery that captivate readers' imaginations. Their relentless pursuit of the truth, even in the face of danger and adversity, embodies themes of perseverance and integrity that have an impact on audiences. Moreover, private investigators often possess a complex blend of strengths and vulnerabilities, making them relatable and multifaceted characters. Readers are drawn to their flaws and inner conflicts, which add depth and authenticity to their narratives, allowing readers to connect with them on a personal level.

What to Watch for When Using the Private Investigator Trope

When incorporating the Private Investigator trope into your novels, there are some key points to keep in mind. These include:

1. **Authenticity**: Maintain realism in portraying the investigative process, including research methods, evidence collection, and legal procedures. Avoid clichés and stereotypes associated with

private investigators, and strive for accuracy in depicting their profession.

2. **Character Depth:** Develop multidimensional characters beyond the investigator's profession, including their motivations, personal history, and relationships. Explore their flaws, vulnerabilities, and moral dilemmas to create compelling and relatable protagonists.

3. **Unique Voice:** Establish a distinct narrative voice for the investigator, reflecting their personality, background, and worldview. Whether they're cynical and world-weary or idealistic and determined, ensure their voice stirs feelings throughout the story.

4. **Plot Complexity:** Craft intricate and engaging mystery plots that challenge both the investigator and the reader. Incorporate twists, red herrings, and unexpected revelations to keep the narrative suspenseful and unpredictable.

5. **Supporting Cast:** Create a diverse cast of supporting characters, including allies, suspects, and antagonists, to enrich the investigative process and provide opportunities for character development and conflict.

6. **Ethical Dilemmas:** Explore ethical dilemmas and moral ambiguity inherent in the investigative profession, such as the use of deception, manipulation, and the pursuit of justice at any cost. Delve into the consequences of the investigator's actions and decisions.

7. **Subverting Tropes:** Avoid falling into predictable tropes and clichés associated with the Private Investigator trope. Instead,

challenge conventions and subvert expectations to keep the narrative fresh and engaging.

By paying attention to these key aspects, you can effectively utilize the Private Investigator trope to craft compelling and nuanced mystery narratives that resonate with readers.

Examples of the Private Investigator Trope

The Private Investigator trope features lone wolves who operate outside the constraints of law enforcement to solve cases and uncover the truth. These enigmatic protagonists often possess a unique blend of street smarts, wit, and determination, making them formidable adversaries for criminals and captivating figures for readers. Following are a few examples of this trope.

- In Alexander McCall Smith's *The No. 1 Ladies' Detective Agency*, Precious Ramotswe, the protagonist of this charming series set in Botswana, epitomizes the Private Investigator trope with her unconventional methods and keen observational skills. As the owner of the titular detective agency, Precious tackles cases ranging from missing persons to marital infidelity, all while navigating the complexities of life in Africa.

- Philip Marlowe, in *The Big Sleep* by Raymond Chandler, is an iconic private eye. He takes center stage in this novel set in 1930s Los Angeles. As he investigates a wealthy family's tangled web of secrets, lies, and murder, Marlowe showcases the gritty determination and moral ambiguity characteristic of the Private Investigator trope. His sharp wit, unflappable demeanor, and willingness to confront corruption and violence make him a timeless figure in the world of mystery fiction.

From gritty urban noir to cozy English villages, the Private Investigator trope continues to captivate readers with its portrayal of resourceful, tenacious protagonists who stop at nothing to uncover the truth. Whether they're navigating the mean streets of Los Angeles or solving crimes in picturesque countryside settings, these enigmatic figures leave an indelible mark on the world of mystery fiction, showcasing the enduring appeal of the lone wolf detective. With their sharp wit, unyielding determination, and unwavering commitment to justice, Private Investigators remind us sometimes, the most compelling mysteries are solved by those who refuse to give up the chase.

Serial Killer Trope
(LT, PP, PT, SKM)

Serial Killer Trope Overview

The Serial Killer trope revolves around a central character who commits a series of murders, typically following a distinct pattern or modus operandi. These killers often possess a compulsion to kill repeatedly, with a signature style or motive that sets them apart from other criminals. The trope is a staple of mystery, thriller, and horror genres, where the pursuit of the serial killer becomes the central focus of the narrative. Protagonists, such as detectives, FBI agents, or amateur sleuths, are tasked with identifying and apprehending the killer before they can strike again, often racing against time to prevent further loss of life. Serial killers are often depicted as cunning and elusive adversaries, leaving behind cryptic clues or taunting messages for law enforcement to decipher. This trope allows storytellers to explore themes of human depravity, the nature of evil, and the psychological impact of violence on both victims and investigators. Additionally, it taps into our collective fascination with true crime and the darker aspects of the human psyche, offering a gripping and suspenseful narrative that keeps audiences hanging on every word.

The Serial Killer trope is commonly found in various mystery sub-genres, each offering a unique context and perspective on this chilling archetype.

One prevalent sub-genre where the Serial Killer trope frequently appears is the Psychological Thriller. In these stories, the focus is on the psychological aspects of the killer's motivations, methods, and the intense cat-and-mouse game between the killer and the protagonist. The exploration of the killer's psyche adds depth and tension to the narrative, keeping readers on tenterhooks as they delve into the darkest corners of the human mind.

Another sub-genre where the Serial Killer trope is prevalent is the Police Procedural. In these novels, the emphasis is on the investigative process, as law enforcement officers work tirelessly to track down and apprehend the elusive killer. The procedural aspects, such as forensic evidence, witness interviews, and profiling techniques, add a layer of authenticity to the story, immersing readers in the intricacies of police work while they unravel the mystery alongside the detectives.

The Serial Killer trope is a versatile and compelling element that can be found across various mystery sub-genres, adding suspense, intrigue, and psychological depth to the narrative. The presence of a serial killer captivates readers and keeps them engrossed in the story as they uncover the truth behind the heinous crimes.

Why Readers Love the Serial Killer Trope

Readers are drawn to the Serial Killer trope for its ability to inspire a complex mix of emotions and sensations that tap into their deepest fears and fascinations. One reason for the trope's popularity is its inherent suspense and tension. The presence of a serial killer introduces an element of danger and unpredictability, keeping readers completely engrossed as they follow the protagonist's journey to uncover the killer's identity and stop their reign of terror. The psychological aspect of the trope, delving into the mind of the killer and exploring their motives and methods, adds an additional layer of intrigue and complexity to the story, enticing readers to unravel the mystery alongside the protagonist.

The Serial Killer trope offers readers a glimpse into the darker aspects of human nature, allowing them to explore themes of morality, justice, and the nature of evil. By delving into the psyche of the killer and examining the factors that drive them to commit such heinous acts, readers are compelled to confront uncomfortable truths about the human condition and society at large. Additionally, the cat-and-mouse dynamic between the killer and the protagonist creates a sense of urgency and suspense that propels the narrative forward, leaving readers eager to uncover the truth and see justice served. Overall, the Serial Killer trope appeals to readers' curiosity, sense of adventure, and desire for thrilling and thought-provoking storytelling, making it a perennial favorite in the mystery genre.

What to Watch for When Using the Serial Killer Trope

Like other tropes, when incorporating the Serial Killer trope into your novels, there are a variety of things you need to watch for. Given the sensitive nature of this trope, these facets are especially important. These include:

1. **Authenticity:** Research is crucial when depicting serial killers in fiction. Strive for authenticity in portraying the psychology, behavior, and motivations of serial killers. This may involve studying real-life cases, consulting experts, and understanding the psychological profiles of serial offenders.

2. **Avoiding Glamorization:** It's important to avoid glorifying or romanticizing serial killers in fiction. Resist the temptation to

sensationalize violence or depict the killer as a charismatic anti-hero. Instead, focus on the impact of their actions on the victims and the community, highlighting the devastating consequences of their crimes.

3. **Balancing Sensitivity and Realism:** While the Serial Killer trope inherently involves dark and disturbing subject matter, approach it with sensitivity and empathy. Be mindful of the potential impact on readers, especially those who may have personal experiences with violence or trauma. Strike a balance between realism and restraint, avoiding gratuitous violence or graphic descriptions that may be triggering or offensive.

4. **Developing Complex Characters:** Both the serial killer and the protagonist should be well-developed, multidimensional characters. Avoid reducing the killer to a one-dimensional stereotype or cliché, and instead, explore their backstory, motivations, and internal conflicts. Similarly, give depth to the protagonist, showing their vulnerabilities, strengths, and moral dilemmas as they pursue the killer.

5. **Subverting Tropes:** While the Serial Killer trope is a staple of the mystery genre, strive to subvert clichés and tropes to keep the narrative fresh and engaging. Experiment with unconventional narrative structures, twists, and character dynamics to challenge readers' expectations and avoid predictability.

When using the Serial Killer trope in your novels, approach it with care, authenticity, and sensitivity. By conducting thorough research, avoiding clichés, and crafting nuanced characters and narratives, you can create compelling stories that explore the complexities of crime, morality, and human nature while respecting the gravity of the subject matter.

Examples of the Serial Killer Trope

The Serial Killer trope is a chilling yet enduring fixture in mystery genre novels, often serving as the dark and menacing force that drives the narrative forward. These sinister figures, driven by twisted motivations and a compulsion to kill, strike fear into the hearts of both characters and readers alike. Let's explore a selection of novels where the Serial Killer takes center stage, terrorizing communities and challenging protagonists to stop their reign of terror.

- Thomas Harris's *The Silence of the Lambs* is perhaps one of the most iconic examples of the Serial Killer trope. This novel introduces readers to Hannibal Lecter, a brilliant psychiatrist and cannibalistic murderer. As FBI trainee Clarice Starling seeks his insight into the mind of another serial killer known as Buffalo Bill, Lecter's chilling intellect and sinister charisma fulfill the trope's expectations, making him a compelling and terrifying antagonist.

- In *The Girl with the Dragon Tattoo* by Stieg Larsson, Lisbeth Salander and journalist Mikael Blomkvist team up to investigate a series of murders spanning several decades. The killer's meticulous planning, sadistic tendencies, and elusive nature embody the traits of the Serial Killer trope, creating a tense and suspenseful atmosphere as the protagonists race against time to stop the murderer before they strike again.

- Francis Dolarhyde is introduced in *Red Dragon* by Thomas Harris. Dolarhyde is a disturbed individual who murders entire families in a ritualistic fashion. Dolarhyde's complex psychology, gruesome rituals, and disturbing past align with the characteristics of the Serial Killer trope, presenting a formidable challenge for FBI profiler Will Graham as he races to apprehend the killer before more lives are lost.

- In *Darkly Dreaming Dexter* by Jeff Lindsay, Dexter Morgan, a blood spatter analyst for the Miami Metro Police Department, leads a double life as a vigilante serial killer targeting criminals who have escaped justice. While Dexter's code of conduct may set him apart from traditional serial killers, his methodical approach to murder and internal struggles with his dark urges fulfill the expectations of the Serial Killer trope, offering readers a unique and morally complex protagonist.

From the calculating genius of Hannibal Lecter to the methodical brutality of Francis Dolarhyde, the Serial Killer trope continues to captivate readers with its portrayal of twisted and malevolent antagonists who strike fear into the hearts of both characters and readers alike. Whether they're driven by psychological trauma, warped ideologies, or insatiable bloodlust, these chilling figures remind us of the darkest depths of the human psyche. With their meticulous planning, sadistic tendencies, and elusive nature, Serial Killers embody the ultimate challenge for protagonists, driving the narrative forward with suspense, tension, and unrelenting dread.

Vigilante Detective Trope
(HBM, NM, STM)

Vigilante Detective Trope Overview

The Vigilante Detective trope is a captivating narrative archetype frequently explored in mystery and crime fiction. This character type typically operates outside the boundaries of traditional law enforcement, driven by a personal sense of justice and a desire to right societal wrongs. Often portrayed as a lone wolf or a small, clandestine group, these detectives take matters into their own hands, disregarding legal protocols and procedures to pursue their version of justice. Motivated by personal vendettas, moral outrage, or a desire to protect the vulnerable, they often confront corruption, crime syndicates, and other forms of injustice conventional authorities cannot or will not address. The Vigilante Detective's actions blur the lines between right and wrong, legality and morality, making them complex and morally ambiguous figures who challenge societal norms while seeking to uphold their own code of ethics.

The Vigilante Detective trope is most commonly found in mystery sub-genres that involve themes of justice, revenge, and moral ambiguity. One such sub-genre is the hard-boiled mystery sub-genre, where gritty and morally ambiguous protagonists often take matters into their own hands to mete out justice. In these stories, the Vigilante Detective may operate outside the boundaries of the law, using unconventional methods to achieve their goals.

Another sub-genre where the Vigilante Detective trope is prevalent is the noir sub-genre. In noir mysteries, the lines between right and wrong are often blurred, and protagonists may resort to vigilantism as a means of addressing perceived injustices. The morally gray nature of noir stories allows for complex characters who are willing to bend or break the rules in pursuit of their version of justice.

Additionally, the Vigilante Detective trope can be found in sub-genres that explore themes of corruption and societal decay, such as suspense thriller mysteries, especially if those have a political or urban slant. In these stories, the protagonist may be driven to vigilantism by a sense of disillusionment with the system or a desire to expose and combat corruption. The Vigilante Detective serves as a symbol of resistance against the forces of injustice, even if their methods are controversial or ethically questionable.

Why Readers Love the Vigilante Detective Trope

Readers are drawn to the Vigilante Detective trope because it appeals to their sense of justice and desire for retribution. In many mystery stories, especially those featuring corrupt officials or unsolved crimes, readers may feel frustrated by the lack of resolution or accountability. The Vigilante Detective offers a cathartic outlet for these feelings, as they take matters into their own hands and deliver swift justice to those who have evaded punishment through conventional means.

Furthermore, the Vigilante Detective often embodies a sense of empowerment and agency that strike a chord with readers. These characters are not content to passively accept the status quo or rely on traditional authorities to uphold justice. Instead, they actively pursue their own brand of justice, often using their intelligence, resourcefulness, and skills to outmaneuver their adversaries. This proactive approach can be both thrilling and inspiring for readers, who may admire the Vigilante Detective's willingness to take risks and challenge the system in pursuit of their ideals.

Overall, the Vigilante Detective trope offers readers a compelling blend of moral complexity, action, and justice. By subverting traditional law enforcement conventions and embracing a more unconventional approach to solving crimes, these characters capture the imagination and keep readers eagerly turning the pages to see how they will navigate the murky waters of morality and bring wrongdoers to account.

What to Watch for When Using the Vigilante Detective Trope

When incorporating the Vigilante Detective trope into your novels, here are some key points to keep in mind:

1. **Character Motivation:** Be certain the Vigilante Detective's motivations for taking the law into their own hands are well-developed and believable. Readers should understand why they feel compelled to pursue justice outside the confines of the legal system.

2. **Moral Complexity:** Explore the moral ambiguity inherent in vigilantism. Portray the ethical dilemmas faced by the Vigilante

Detective as they navigate the fine line between right and wrong, legality and justice.

3. **Realistic Consequences:** Depict the potential consequences of the Vigilante Detective's actions, both for themselves and for those around them. Consider the legal, social, and personal ramifications of their vigilantism.

4. **Character Development:** Use the Vigilante Detective's journey as an opportunity for character growth and development. Show how their experiences shape their worldview, beliefs, and relationships over the course of the story.

5. **Contextualization:** Situate the Vigilante Detective within a richly detailed and believable world. Consider the socio-political context in which they operate and how this influences their actions and decisions.

6. **Avoiding Clichés:** Strive to avoid clichéd portrayals of the Vigilante Detective archetype. Look for fresh and original ways to depict their character, motivations, and methods.

7. **Ethical Considerations:** Prompt readers to consider the ethical implications of vigilantism and the broader issues of justice and accountability raised by the trope.

The Vigilante Detective trope can add depth, intrigue, and moral complexity to mystery novels when used thoughtfully and skillfully. By addressing these key considerations, you can effectively harness the power of this trope to create compelling narratives that connect with readers.

Examples of the Vigilante Detective Trope

The Vigilante Detective trope introduces protagonists who take the law into their own hands, driven by a sense of justice and a desire to right the wrongs they perceive in society. These characters often operate outside the boundaries of conventional law enforcement, using their own methods to mete out justice to criminals. Here are some examples of novels where the Vigilante Detective takes center stage, challenging readers to grapple with questions of morality, ethics, and the nature of justice.

- In the *Jack Reacher* series by Lee Child, Jack Reacher is a former military police officer turned drifter. He becomes a vigilante detective in his quest for justice across the United States. Armed with his keen investigative instincts and formidable combat skills, Reacher intervenes in cases of injustice and corruption, often taking matters into his own hands to protect the innocent and punish wrongdoers, epitomizing the archetype of the Vigilante Detective.

- In *The Reversal* by Michael Connelly, defense attorney Mickey Haller teams up with LAPD detective Harry Bosch to investigate a high-profile case involving a convicted child molester seeking exoneration. While Haller operates within the legal system, Bosch's uncompromising pursuit of justice often leads him to adopt the role of a vigilante detective, bending the rules to guarantee the guilty are held accountable and the innocent are protected.

- After his wife is murdered and his daughter sexually assaulted, Paul Benjamin takes on the role of a vigilante detective, in *Death Wish* by Brian Garfield. He seeks vengeance against the criminals responsible for his family's suffering. Armed with a .32 caliber revolver, Benjamin embarks on a relentless quest for justice, targeting violent criminals and corrupt officials in a gritty portrayal of vigilantism and its consequences.

The Vigilante Detective trope offers readers a compelling exploration of justice, morality, and the human desire for retribution in the face of injustice. Whether they're driven by personal vendettas, moral convictions, or a quest for vengeance, these characters challenge the boundaries of law and order, often operating outside the constraints of conventional justice systems. With their unyielding pursuit of truth and their willingness to confront corruption and wrongdoing head-on, Vigilante Detectives captivate readers with their moral complexity, their unwavering determination, and their relentless quest for justice in a world plagued by crime and corruption.

CHAPTER 6:

Setting Tropes for the Mystery Genre

Setting tropes offer writers a powerful tool for immersing readers in the world of their story and enhancing the narrative experience. By leveraging familiar and recognizable settings, such as the "Small Town" or "Urban Jungle," writers can establish a strong sense of place that rings true with readers on a personal level. These tropes provide a backdrop against which characters can interact, conflicts can unfold, and mysteries can unravel, grounding the story in a rich and vivid environment.

Setting tropes serve to establish the tone and atmosphere of a narrative, setting the stage for the events that transpire within it. For example, the "Haunted House" trope immediately invokes feelings of suspense, fear, and unease, signaling to readers they are in for a thrilling and potentially chilling ride. Similarly, the "Isolated Cabin" trope suggests seclusion, isolation, and vulnerability, creating the perfect setting for a suspenseful and claustrophobic mystery.

Additionally, setting tropes can function as storytelling shorthand, allowing writers to convey key information about the world of their story efficiently and effectively. Rather than spending pages describing the physical characteristics of a setting, writers can rely on familiar tropes to establish the necessary context and background, freeing up valuable space for character development, plot progression, and thematic exploration. In this way, setting tropes not only enhance the immersive quality of a narrative but also streamline the storytelling process, making it easier for writers to craft compelling and engaging stories.

Haunted House Trope
(CM, GM, OM, PM)

The Haunted House trope is a classic element of mystery and horror storytelling, featuring a residence imbued with supernatural phenomena and malevolent spirits. Typically, the haunted house serves as the primary setting for the narrative, presenting an eerie and foreboding atmosphere that kindles feelings of fear and dread. Characters who inhabit or venture into the haunted abode often encounter unexplained occurrences such as ghostly apparitions, mysterious noises, and inexplicable events. As the story unfolds, the protagonists may uncover dark secrets or tragic events from the house's past, revealing the source of the haunting. Themes of isolation, madness, and the thin veil between the living and the dead are prevalent, heightening the suspense and tension as characters confront the sinister forces within the haunted house.

The Haunted House trope is a classic element of mystery and horror fiction, often found in various sub-genres that explore the intersection of the supernatural and the mysterious. One common setting where this trope is prevalent is in the Gothic mystery sub-genre. In these stories, the haunted house serves as a central focal point, shrouded in dark secrets and unsettling mysteries. Characters are drawn to the house out of curiosity or necessity, only to uncover sinister truths lurking within its walls.

The Haunted House trope also frequently appears in the paranormal mystery sub-genre. In these stories, the haunted house is not just a physical location but a nexus of paranormal activity, where spirits, ghosts, or other supernatural entities manifest. Investigators must navigate the eerie atmosphere of the house while unraveling the mysteries of its haunted past and confronting the supernatural forces at play.

Additionally, the Haunted House trope often features prominently in the cozy mystery sub-genre (as well as the paranormal cozy subset of this sub-genre), albeit with a lighter and more whimsical tone. In these stories, the haunted house may be a quaint and charming old mansion, inhabited by friendly ghosts or quirky spirits. While the mysteries may be less intense, the presence of the haunted house adds an element of intrigue and whimsy to the narrative, keeping readers engaged and entertained.

No matter which sub-genre the Haunted House finds itself in, its presence adds an extra layer of mystery and suspense to the narrative, inviting readers into a world where the line between the natural and the supernatural is blurred, and secrets lurk behind every creaking floorboard.

Why Readers Love the Haunted House Trope

The Haunted House trope ellicits a sense of mystery, suspense, and fear, which many readers love. The allure of the unknown and the supernatural holds a powerful fascination for many, and the haunted house serves as a tangible manifestation of these elements. Its presence in a story promises thrills and chills, tapping into primal fears of the unseen and the unexplained.

This trope also often provides a rich backdrop for exploring themes of trauma, grief, and unresolved pasts. The house itself becomes a character, reflecting the emotional turmoil of its inhabitants and serving as a metaphor for the haunted memories that linger within. Readers are intrigued by the layers of history and hidden secrets waiting to be uncovered, adding depth and complexity to the narrative.

Additionally, the Haunted House trope offers a compelling blend of psychological and supernatural horror. The uncertainty of what lies behind each creaking floorboard or shadowy corner keeps readers on edge, heightening the tension and suspense. Whether it's a malevolent spirit seeking vengeance or a tragic ghost trapped in limbo, the haunting presence adds an element of unpredictability and danger to the story, keeping readers eagerly turning the pages.

Readers love the Haunted House trope for its ability to captivate the imagination, rouse primal fears, and provide a rich tapestry for exploring themes of trauma and the supernatural. Its presence in a mystery narrative adds depth, intrigue, and suspense, making it a beloved and enduring element of the genre.

What to Watch for When Using the Haunted House Trope

While your haunted house in your novel may set the scene for twists and turns and surprises in your story readers should look out for, the Haunted House trope also has things you, as the writer, need to watch for. These include:

1. **Establish Atmosphere:** Create a vivid and immersive atmosphere that enhances the sense of dread and unease surrounding the haunted house. Use descriptive language to spark the setting's eerie ambiance, incorporating details such as creaking floorboards, flickering lights, and cold drafts to set the scene.

2. **Develop the Haunting:** Develop the haunting itself, whether it's caused by a malevolent spirit, a tragic ghost, or some other supernatural force. Provide clues and hints throughout the narrative to gradually reveal the nature of the haunting and its impact on the characters and the house itself.

3. **Build Tension:** Build tension steadily throughout the story, leveraging the uncertainty and mystery surrounding the haunted house to keep readers engaged. Employ pacing techniques such as foreshadowing, suspenseful encounters, and escalating supernatural occurrences to maintain a sense of urgency and unease.

4. **Explore Themes:** Use the haunted house as a means to explore deeper themes such as trauma, grief, guilt, and the nature of evil. Consider how the haunting reflects the psychological and emotional struggles of the characters, as well as the larger societal or historical context in which the house exists.

5. **Subvert Expectations:** While the Haunted House trope has certain conventions, strive to subvert expectations and offer fresh twists on familiar tropes. Avoid relying too heavily on clichés and stereotypes, instead infusing the narrative with originality and unpredictability to keep readers guessing.

In the end, approach the Haunted House trope with careful consideration and attention to detail, focusing on establishing atmosphere, developing the haunting, building tension, exploring themes, and subverting expectations to create a compelling and memorable narrative.

Examples of the Haunted House Trope

The Haunted House trope intertwines elements of suspense, horror, and psychological intrigue, weaving tales of spectral encounters and haunted histories that captivate readers' imaginations. Following are a selection of mystery books that feature the Haunted House trope, each offering a unique and chilling exploration of the paranormal.

- *The Haunting of Bechdel Mansion* by Roger Hayden utilizes the classic Haunted House trope to create a suspenseful and chilling atmosphere. As the protagonist explores the mysterious Bechdel Mansion, they uncover dark secrets and encounter paranormal phenomena, heightening the sense of fear and intrigue for both the characters and the reader. Through the Haunted House motif, Hayden effectively builds tension and explores themes of the supernatural and the unknown.

- *The Curse of the House on Cypress Lane* by James Hunt employs the Haunted House trope to weave a tale of suspense and terror. As the characters grapple with the dark history of the house, they confront malevolent spirits and unearth unsettling truths, intensifying the atmosphere of dread and mystery. Through the Haunted House motif, Hunt crafts a gripping narrative that explores themes of haunting, redemption, and the sinister forces that dwell within the shadows.

- *Sleeping Murder* by Agatha Christie ingeniously incorporates the Haunted House trope into a classic murder mystery. As the protagonist investigates the seemingly innocuous house she purchases, she is confronted with eerie occurrences and a pervasive sense of dread, leading her to uncover a long-buried secret and solve a decades-old murder. Christie masterfully uses the Haunted House motif to heighten suspense and intrigue, blending elements of the supernatural with her trademark twists and turns.

Isolated Cabin Trope
(PT, W)

The Isolated Cabin trope is a classic element of mystery fiction, often serving as a secluded and atmospheric setting for suspenseful tales of intrigue and danger. Nestled deep in the wilderness, far from civilization and modern conveniences, the isolated cabin stimulates feelings of isolation, vulnerability, and claustrophobia. Its remote location creates a sense of foreboding and unease, making it the perfect backdrop for mysteries where characters are cut off from help and must confront their fears in a hostile environment. The cabin's rustic charm may hide dark secrets lurking within its walls, and its isolated setting adds an extra layer of tension as characters navigate the treacherous terrain and confront unknown threats lurking in the shadows. Whether it's a retreat gone wrong or a desperate escape from danger, the Isolated Cabin trope offers endless possibilities for suspenseful storytelling in the mystery genre.

The Isolated Cabin trope is commonly found in various sub-genres of mystery fiction, each utilizing its atmospheric setting to enhance the tension and suspense of the narrative. In traditional whodunit mysteries, the isolated cabin often serves as the scene of the crime, where a group of suspects is trapped together and must unravel the mystery before the killer strikes again. This sub-genre relies on the confined space of the cabin to heighten suspicion and build a sense of paranoia among the characters.

In psychological thrillers, the isolated cabin trope is frequently employed to explore themes of isolation and psychological torment. Characters may find themselves stranded in the wilderness with no means of escape, forced to confront their inner demons and dark secrets while battling external threats. The remote setting of the cabin amplifies the psychological tension, creating a sense of confinement and increasing the stakes for the characters as they struggle to survive.

Overall, the isolated cabin trope adds depth and complexity to mystery narratives by providing a richly atmospheric setting that amplifies the suspense and intrigue of the story. Its remote location and confined space create a sense of claustrophobia and vulnerability, driving the tension forward as characters grapple with external threats and internal conflicts amidst the isolation of the wilderness.

Why Readers Love the Isolated Cabin Trope

Readers enjoy the Isolated Cabin trope in mystery fiction for its ability to create a tense and atmospheric setting that heightens the sense of suspense and intrigue. The remote and secluded nature of the cabin evokes a feeling of isolation and vulnerability, trapping characters in a confined space with limited resources and no easy means of escape. This sense of confinement intensifies the stakes of the story, as characters are forced to confront their fears and confront the unknown dangers lurking in the wilderness.

Additionally, the Isolated Cabin trope often serves as a catalyst for character development and exploration of psychological themes. As characters are thrust into unfamiliar and perilous situations, they must confront their inner demons, face their past traumas, and grapple with moral dilemmas in order to survive. This allows readers to delve deeper into the psyche of the characters and witness their transformation as they navigate the challenges of the isolated cabin setting. Overall, readers are captivated by the Isolated Cabin trope because it provides a richly atmospheric backdrop for mystery narratives, blending elements of suspense, survival, and psychological tension to create a compelling and immersive reading experience.

What to Watch for When Using the Isolated Cabin Trope

When incorporating the Isolated Cabin trope into your novel, be mindful of the items below to guarantee you're using it effectively.

1. **Establish the Atmosphere:** Begin by vividly describing the secluded setting of the cabin, emphasizing its remoteness, eerie silence, and isolation from civilization. Use sensory details to prompts a sense of foreboding and unease, setting the stage for suspenseful events to unfold.

2. **Develop the Characters:** Introduce a diverse cast of characters with distinct personalities, backgrounds, and motivations. Consider how the isolation of the cabin will affect each character differently, amplifying tensions and interpersonal dynamics. Use the confined space to explore the depths of their relationships and conflicts.

3. **Build Tension Gradually:** Employ suspenseful pacing and subtle foreshadowing to create a sense of mounting dread as the characters realize they are not alone in the cabin. Introduce mysterious occurrences, unexplained noises, and unsettling discoveries to keep readers on edge and eager to uncover the truth.

4. **Utilize the Environment:** Take full advantage of the isolated cabin setting to heighten the sense of danger and unpredictability. Use the surrounding wilderness as both a refuge and a threat, with natural elements such as harsh weather, dense forests, and rugged terrain posing additional challenges to the characters' survival.

5. **Subvert Expectations**: While the Isolated Cabin trope may seem familiar, strive to inject fresh twists and unexpected revelations into the narrative. Subvert genre conventions and challenge readers' assumptions by introducing surprising plot developments, complex moral dilemmas, and morally ambiguous characters.

Paying attention to these items will help you effectively leverage the Isolated Cabin trope to create a gripping and atmospheric mystery novel that keeps readers enthralled from start to finish.

Examples of the Isolated Cabin Trope

Secluded from the outside world, in the Isolated Cabin trope, cabins become microcosms of danger, where characters must confront their deepest fears and darkest secrets. Here are some examples of mystery genre books that skillfully utilize the Isolated Cabin trope to captivate readers with their gripping narratives.

- In *The Girl with the Dragon Tattoo* by Stieg Larsson, journalist Mikael Blomkvist retreats to a remote cabin to investigate a decades-old disappearance. As he delves into the case, he discovers the isolation of the cabin mirrors the isolation of the victim's family, creating an atmosphere of suspicion and paranoia that keeps readers rivetted to the story.

- In *The Woman in Cabin 10* by Ruth Ware, the Isolated Cabin trope takes on a sea-faring twist. When travel journalist Lo Blacklock witnesses a murder aboard a luxury cruise ship, she finds herself trapped in a cabin, isolated from the rest of the passengers. As tensions rise and suspicions mount, the claustrophobic setting of the cabin amplifies the sense of danger and uncertainty, making every revelation more chilling than the last.

- *And Then There Were None* by Agatha Christie expands the Isolated Cabin trope to an isolated mansion on a secluded island. In this classic mystery novel, ten strangers are lured to the island under false pretenses, where they become stranded. As they are picked off one by one by an unknown assailant, the isolated cabin setting heightens the sense of paranoia and distrust among the characters, leading to a shocking and unforgettable conclusion.

- A group of old friends gather at a remote Scottish lodge for a New Year's Eve celebration, only to find themselves snowed in and cut off from the outside world in *The Hunting Party* by Lucy Foley. As tensions simmer and long-buried secrets come to light, the isolation of the cabin intensifies the suspense and drives the characters to desperate measures in their fight for survival.

From remote islands to snowbound lodges, the Isolated Cabin trope continues to captivate readers with its atmospheric tension and claustrophobic suspense. Whether it's used to heighten the sense of danger or to explore the darker aspects of human nature, these mystery genre books demonstrate the enduring power of the Isolated Cabin setting to keep readers enthralled until the final page.

Locked Room Trope
(CM, HM, PT, W)

Locked Room Trope Overview

The Locked Room trope is a classic mystery element where a crime, typically a murder, occurs in a room or location that appears to be completely sealed off from the outside world. Despite the apparent impossibility of entry or exit, a crime is committed, leaving investigators baffled and readers intrigued. This trope challenges both the characters and the audience to unravel the mystery of how the perpetrator gained access to the locked room and committed the crime without leaving any trace. It often requires a keen eye for detail, creative problem-solving, and an understanding of human behavior to solve. The Locked Room trope adds an extra layer of complexity and intrigue to mystery narratives, as characters must navigate through a web of clues and red herrings to uncover the truth behind the seemingly impossible crime.

The Locked Room trope is most often found in various sub-genres of mystery fiction, where it serves as a classic plot device to create intrigue and challenge the protagonist's investigative skills. One prominent sub-genre where this trope is frequently employed is the traditional whodunit mystery. In these stories, a murder occurs in a seemingly impenetrable location, such as a sealed room or a secured building, leaving the detective and readers perplexed as to how the crime could have been committed. The challenge of unraveling the mystery within the confines of the locked room adds complexity to the investigation and often leads to ingenious solutions.

The Locked Room trope is also prevalent is the psychological thriller. In these stories, the locked room serves as a metaphorical representation of the protagonist's mind or subconscious, where they must confront their deepest fears or secrets. The confined space heightens the sense of psychological tension and suspense, as the protagonist grapples with their inner demons while also navigating external threats.

Additionally, the Locked Room trope is commonly used in the cozy mystery sub-genre, where it provides a cozy yet perplexing puzzle for amateur sleuths to solve. In these lighthearted mysteries, the locked room often serves as the focal point of the investigation, inviting readers to engage in the challenge of piecing together clues and uncovering the truth behind the seemingly impossible crime. The trope adds an element of intrigue and intellectual stimulation to the cozy mystery narrative, making it a beloved staple of the genre.

Overall, the Locked Room trope is a versatile and enduring setting trope that can be adapted to various sub-genres of mystery fiction, providing you with a rich source of inspiration for crafting compelling and suspenseful narratives.

Why Readers Love the Locked Room Trope

The Locked Room trope captivates readers for several reasons, drawing them into the mystery and intrigue of seemingly impossible situations. Firstly, this trope offers a unique and challenging puzzle for both the characters and the readers to unravel. The idea of a locked room or sealed environment immediately sets the stage for an intricate mystery, prompting readers to engage in the investigation alongside the protagonist. The sense of curiosity and anticipation surrounding how the crime was committed in such a restricted space compels readers to keep turning the pages in search of answers.

It creates an atmosphere of suspense and tension that enhances the overall reading experience. The confined setting, whether it's a sealed chamber, a remote cabin, or a locked mansion, heightens the stakes of the investigation and amplifies the sense of danger faced by the characters. Readers are drawn into the claustrophobic environment, eagerly anticipating the moment when the truth behind the locked room will be revealed. This tension keeps readers holding their literary breath, eager to uncover the secrets hidden within the confined space.

This trope allows for creative and imaginative storytelling, as you must devise clever and plausible explanations for how the crime could have been committed under seemingly impossible circumstances. This challenge encourages you to think outside the box and craft inventive solutions that surprise and delight readers. The ingenuity required to construct a compelling locked room mystery adds an extra layer of enjoyment for readers, who appreciate the intricacy and cleverness of the narrative puzzle.

Readers are drawn to the Locked Room trope for its ability to present them with a tantalizing mystery, create suspenseful and immersive environments, and inspire creative storytelling. By engaging readers' curiosity, heightening tension, and encouraging imaginative problem-solving, this trope has become a beloved and enduring element of mystery fiction that continues to captivate audiences across generations.

What to Watch for When Using the Locked Room Trope

The Locked Room trope is a classic element of mystery fiction that adds intrigue and complexity to the narrative. However, its effective use requires careful consideration to avoid clichés and maintain reader engagement. Here are some key points to keep in mind when incorporating the Locked Room trope into your novels:

1. **Originality is Key:** While the Locked Room trope has been used in countless mystery stories, strive to put a fresh spin on it. Avoid relying on predictable scenarios and instead brainstorm unique and inventive ways to create the locked room mystery.

2. **Establish Plausibility:** One challenge of the Locked Room trope is maintaining believability. Ensure the circumstances leading to the locked room scenario are plausible within the context of your story world. Readers should be able to suspend their disbelief without feeling the setup is contrived.

3. **Balance Puzzle and Storytelling:** While the puzzle aspect of the locked room mystery is essential, don't let it overshadow character development and plot progression. Integrate the locked room scenario seamlessly into the broader narrative, using it as a catalyst for character growth and thematic exploration.

4. **Subvert Expectations:** Surprise your readers by subverting traditional conventions associated with the Locked Room trope. Consider flipping the script on who the victim or perpetrator is, or introducing unexpected elements that challenge the protagonist's assumptions and investigative techniques.

5. **Foreshadowing and Clues:** Provide subtle clues and foreshadowing throughout the story to hint at the solution to the locked room mystery. Cleverly planted hints will engage readers and allow them to participate in solving the puzzle alongside the protagonist.

6. **Avoid Over-Explanation:** While it's important to provide a satisfying resolution to the locked room mystery, avoid excessive exposition or spoon-feeding the solution to readers. Trust your audience to piece together the clues and come to their own conclusions, respecting their intelligence and deductive abilities.

These guidelines will help you use the Locked Room trope to create captivating and memorable mysteries that will keep readers guessing until the very end.

Examples of the Locked Room Trope

The Locked Room trope adds an extra layer of intrigue and complexity to the plot. In these stories, a crime is committed in a seemingly impossible situation, such as a room that is locked from the inside with no apparent way for the perpetrator to escape. Following are books that skillfully employ the Locked Room trope to challenge readers and keep them guessing until the very end.

- In the iconic novel, *The Murder of Roger Ackroyd* by Agatha Christie, Hercule Poirot investigates the murder of Roger Ackroyd in his locked study. The setting fulfills the Locked Room trope by presenting a scenario where the killer seemingly vanishes into thin air, leaving Poirot to unravel the intricate web of lies and deception surrounding the crime.

- Considered one of the earliest examples of the Locked Room trope, *The Mystery of the Yellow Room* by Gaston Leroux follows detective Joseph Rouletabille as he investigates the attempted murder of a young woman in her locked bedroom. The novel expertly fulfills the trope by presenting a baffling puzzle that seems impossible to solve, challenging Rouletabille to use his deductive skills to uncover the truth.

- In *The Locked Room* by Maj Sjöwall and Per Wahlöö, a man is found dead inside a locked room with no apparent cause of death. As Beck and his team investigate, they uncover a tangled web of family secrets and betrayals, fulfilling the Locked Room trope by presenting a seemingly unsolvable mystery that challenges their investigative skills.

The Locked Room trope continues to captivate readers with its clever puzzles and seemingly impossible crimes. The books above demonstrate the enduring appeal of the Locked Room setting in keeping readers enthralled until the final revelation.

Small Town Mystery Trope (AS, CM, PM, PP, PT, STM, W)

Small Town Trope Overview

The Small Town trope is a narrative device commonly employed in mystery fiction, characterized by setting the story in a quaint or secluded town where everyone knows everyone else's business—or so it seems. Behind the facade of idyllic charm and neighborly camaraderie lies a dark underbelly of secrets, scandals, and unsolved crimes. In these settings, seemingly ordinary townsfolk become suspects, and the close-knit community dynamics add layers of intrigue and suspicion to the plot. As an investigator—whether amateur sleuth, seasoned detective, or curious outsider—begins to unravel the mysteries lurking beneath the surface, they encounter resistance from locals keen on protecting their town's reputation or hiding their own involvement. The Small Town trope often explores themes of loyalty, betrayal, and the clash between appearances and reality, offering readers a compelling blend of suspense and familiarity as they navigate the twists and turns of the story's setting.

The Small Town trope is a versatile element commonly found across various sub-genres of mystery fiction, each with its own unique spin on the classic setting. In traditional or cozy mysteries, small towns serve as idyllic backdrops for quaint and charming communities where everyone knows each other's business. These settings offer a sense of intimacy and familiarity, where secrets are hard to keep and mysteries are often solved by astute amateur sleuths or quirky local detectives. The close-knit nature of small towns provides ample opportunities for character development and interpersonal drama, adding depth and richness to the narrative.

In police procedurals, small towns present a stark contrast to the bustling urban environments typically associated with crime dramas. Here, law enforcement officers navigate the complexities of rural life while investigating crimes that disrupt the peace and tranquility of the community. The close ties between residents and the local police force can complicate investigations, as personal loyalties and longstanding grudges come into play. The small-town setting lends itself to gritty and realistic portrayals of crime and justice in tight-knit communities, where everyone has something to hide.

In psychological thrillers and suspense thriller mysteries, small towns take on a darker and more sinister tone, becoming hotbeds of secrets, scandals, and hidden agendas. Behind the picturesque facade lies a web of intrigue and deception, where dark secrets lurk beneath the surface and danger lurks around every corner. The isolation of small-town life can heighten feelings of paranoia and claustrophobia, amplifying the psychological tension and suspense of the narrative. In these stories, the small-town setting becomes a character in its own right, shaping the actions and motivations of the individuals who inhabit it.

The Small Town trope is a versatile and evocative element of mystery fiction, offering a rich and fertile landscape in which to explore the intricacies of human nature, relationships, and society. Whether used as a backdrop for cozy mysteries, police procedurals, or psychological thrillers, small towns provide endless opportunities for storytelling and intrigue, making them a perennial favorite among readers of mystery fiction.

Why Readers Love the Small Town Trope

Readers enjoy the Small Town trope in mystery fiction for its captivating blend of charm, intimacy, and intrigue. One of the primary reasons for its appeal is the sense of nostalgia and comfort it stirs. Small towns often embody a simpler way of life, where neighbors know each other by name, and the pace of life is more relaxed. This nostalgic allure touches a nerve with readers who long for a sense of community and belonging, making them feel connected to the characters and their surroundings.

Moreover, small towns provide a rich tapestry of characters and relationships for you to explore. From quirky shop owners to nosy neighbors and colorful local personalities, the diverse cast of characters adds depth and authenticity to the narrative. Readers enjoy getting to know the residents of the small town, each with their own secrets, quirks, and motives. This rich characterization adds layers of complexity to the story, making it more engaging and immersive.

The small-town setting lends itself to compelling mysteries and intricate plotlines. In a close-knit community where everyone knows each other's business, even the smallest of secrets can have far-reaching consequences. This creates a fertile ground for conflict, drama, and suspense, as characters navigate the tangled web of relationships and uncover long-buried secrets. Readers are intrigued by the challenge of unraveling the mysteries hidden beneath the surface of the seemingly tranquil small town, keeping them eagerly turning the pages to uncover the truth.

The juxtaposition of the idyllic small-town setting with the darker elements of crime and mystery adds tension and suspense to the narrative. The contrast between the quaint facade of the town and the sinister underbelly of crime creates a sense of unease and foreboding, keeping readers captivated by the narrative. This blend of charm and danger creates a compelling atmosphere that draws readers in and keeps them invested in the story until the very end. Overall, the Small Town trope offers a captivating blend of nostalgia, rich characterization, and suspense that stirs feelings with readers and keeps them coming back for more.

What to Watch for When Using the Small Town Trope

Using the Small Town trope in a mystery novel can add depth and richness to the story, but be mindful of certain pitfalls to avoid. Here are some to keep in mind:

1. **Think Outside the Box**: While small towns offer a wealth of storytelling opportunities, it's essential to steer clear of clichés and stereotypes. Instead of relying on tired tropes, strive to create nuanced and authentic portrayals of small-town life and characters.

2. **Balanced Characterization:** When populating your small town with characters, be certain they are well-rounded and multifaceted. Avoid falling into the trap of making characters overly idealized or one-dimensional. Give them depth, flaws, and motivations that feel true to life.

3. **Maintain Realism:** While small towns often have a cozy and picturesque charm, they are not immune to real-world issues. Be mindful of portraying the darker aspects of small-town life, such

as social tensions, economic struggles, and interpersonal conflicts, with sensitivity and realism.

4. **Respect the Setting:** Treat the small town itself as a character in the story, with its own history, quirks, and atmosphere. Pay attention to the details of the setting, from its geography and architecture to its local customs and traditions. Make the town feel alive and vibrant, adding depth and texture to the narrative.

5. **Avoid Overly Simplistic Plots:** While small towns may seem idyllic on the surface, they can harbor complex and intricate mysteries. Avoid falling into the trap of overly simplistic plots or predictable storylines. Instead, challenge readers with twists, turns, and unexpected revelations that keep them guessing until the end.

While the Small Town trope can be a powerful tool for crafting compelling mysteries, you must approach it with care and attention to detail. By avoiding clichés, creating nuanced characters, maintaining realism, respecting the setting, and crafting complex plots, you can harness the full potential of the Small Town trope to create immersive and engaging stories that resonate with readers.

Examples of the Small Town Trope

The Small Town trope is a quintessential element of mystery fiction, often serving as the backdrop for tales of secrets, intrigue, and dark deeds lurking beneath the surface of idyllic communities. In these stories, the close-knit nature of small towns creates a fertile ground for suspenseful narratives, where everyone knows everyone else's business, and the line between friend and foe becomes blurred. Here are some examples of mystery genre books that skillfully utilize the Small Town trope to immerse readers in gripping tales of crime and deception.

- In *Sharp Objects* by Gillian Flynn, journalist Camille Preaker returns to her hometown of Wind Gap to investigate the murders of two young girls. The small-town setting of Wind Gap highlights the claustrophobic atmosphere and deep-rooted secrets that permeate every corner of the community, leading Camille to confront her own troubled past in the process.

- Set in the affluent coastal town of Monterey, California, *Big Little Lies* by Liane Moriarty follows a group of women whose lives intertwine amidst scandal and betrayal. The small-town setting of Monterey serves as the perfect backdrop for the novel's exploration of social dynamics and the facade of perfection, as the characters navigate the murky waters of friendship, rivalry, and deception.

- In *In the Woods* by Tana French, Detective Rob Ryan returns to his hometown of Knocknaree to investigate the murder of a young girl, triggering memories of his own childhood trauma. The small-town setting of Knocknaree fulfills the trope by emphasizing the close-knit community and the haunting secrets hidden beneath its picturesque exterior, as Rob grapples with the demons of his past while unraveling the mystery of the present.

The Small Town trope continues to be a cornerstone of mystery fiction, offering authors a rich tapestry of characters and settings to explore. The Small Town setting captivates readers with tales of crime, betrayal, and redemption.

Urban Jungle Trope
(FM, HBM, NM, PP, SKM)

Urban Jungle Trope Overview

The Urban Jungle trope in the mystery genre refers to stories set in bustling, metropolitan environments characterized by towering skyscrapers, crowded streets, and a palpable sense of anonymity and alienation. In these narratives, the city itself often functions as a central character, with its labyrinthine streets and shadowy alleyways serving as the backdrop for thrilling investigations and dangerous encounters. The Urban Jungle trope explores themes of urban decay, corruption, and moral ambiguity, highlighting the darker underbelly of city life while also showcasing the resilience and resourcefulness of its inhabitants. From gritty detective stories to high-stakes thrillers, the Urban Jungle trope offers a rich and dynamic setting that adds depth and complexity to mystery narratives.

The Urban Jungle trope is most often found in mystery sub-genres that emphasize the gritty and chaotic nature of urban environments. One such sub-genre is the hard-boiled mystery, where protagonists navigate the mean streets of cities like Los Angeles or New York, uncovering corruption and unraveling complex conspiracies. In these stories, the urban setting serves as a reflection of the protagonist's tough exterior and cynical worldview, with neon-lit alleyways and dimly-lit bars adding to the atmosphere of danger and intrigue.

Another sub-genre where the Urban Jungle trope thrives is the police procedural, where law enforcement officers investigate crimes in bustling urban centers. From homicide detectives combing through crime scenes to beat cops patrolling city streets, these stories delve into the intricacies of urban law enforcement and the challenges of maintaining order in a metropolis teeming with criminal activity. The urban setting provides a rich backdrop for police investigations, with its diverse population and complex social dynamics adding depth to the narrative.

Unsurprisingly, the Urban Jungle trope is commonly featured in noir mystery sub-genre, where morally ambiguous protagonists navigate the seedy underbelly of urban life. These stories often explore themes of corruption, betrayal, and existential despair, with the city itself serving as a metaphor for the protagonist's inner turmoil. From dilapidated tenements to glitzy nightclubs, the urban setting in noir mystery is rife with danger and temptation, offering a compelling backdrop for tales of crime and redemption.

Why Readers Love the Urban Jungle Trope

Readers are drawn to the Urban Jungle trope for its gritty realism and immersive atmosphere. The portrayal of urban environments as sprawling, chaotic landscapes filled with both beauty and danger connects with audiences who enjoy stories that reflect the complexities of modern society. The vibrant energy of city life, with its bustling streets, towering skyscrapers, and diverse population, provides a rich tapestry for storytelling, inviting readers to explore the intricacies of urban culture and the human experience.

Furthermore, the Urban Jungle trope often serves as a backdrop for compelling character-driven narratives. Protagonists navigating the streets of a bustling metropolis must confront their inner demons while grappling with external challenges, creating opportunities for rich character development and emotional depth. Whether they are hardened detectives solving crimes, vigilante heroes seeking justice, or ordinary citizens navigating the urban landscape, readers are drawn to characters who face adversity head-on in the concrete jungle, making the Urban Jungle trope a perennial favorite in mystery fiction.

What to Watch for When Using the Urban Jungle Trope

To use the Urban Jungle effectively, it's important to consider a few things. These include:

1. **Establish Atmosphere:** The urban setting should be vividly depicted to immerse readers in the bustling streets, towering skyscrapers, and diverse neighborhoods of the city. Use descriptive language to inspire the sights, sounds, and smells of the urban environment, creating a sense of place that enhances the narrative.

2. **Explore Diversity:** Cities are melting pots of cultures, languages, and lifestyles, offering a wealth of opportunities to explore diversity in your stories. Include characters from various backgrounds and perspectives to reflect the rich tapestry of urban life and add depth to the narrative.

3. **Navigate Social Issues:** The Urban Jungle trope provides a platform for addressing important social issues such as crime, poverty, gentrification, and inequality. Handle these themes with sensitivity and nuance, using your stories to shed light on pressing societal concerns and provoke thought-provoking discussions.

4. **Utilize Urban Legends:** Cities are often steeped in folklore, urban legends, and myths that add an air of mystery and intrigue to the narrative. Incorporate elements of local lore and legend into the story to captivate readers and add an extra layer of depth to the urban setting.

5. **Balance Realism with Escapism:** While realism is key to portraying the gritty authenticity of the urban environment, allow room for escapism and fantasy. Strike a balance between gritty realism and imaginative storytelling to keep readers engaged and entertained throughout the narrative.

The Urban Jungle trope offers a rich and dynamic backdrop for mystery fiction, providing ample opportunities for immersive world-building, diverse character development, and thought-provoking exploration of social issues. By paying attention to atmosphere, diversity, social issues, urban legends, and balancing realism with escapism, you can effectively leverage the Urban Jungle trope to create compelling and memorable stories that strikes a chord with readers.

Examples of the Urban Jungle Trope

The Urban Jungle trope is a compelling element of mystery fiction, portraying cities as vibrant yet dangerous landscapes where crime lurks around every corner. In these stories, the bustling streets, towering skyscrapers, and labyrinthine alleys become integral parts of the narrative, shaping the characters' experiences and influencing the unfolding of the plot. Following are a few examples of mystery genre books that skillfully utilize the Urban Jungle trope to immerse readers in thrilling tales of intrigue and suspense.

- Set in the urban sprawl of Stockholm, Sweden, *The Girl with the Dragon Tattoo* by Stieg Larsson follows journalist Mikael Blomkvist and hacker Lisbeth Salander as they investigate the disappearance of a young woman. The Urban Jungle setting of Stockholm portrays the city as a gritty and dangerous landscape where corruption and crime thrive, adding depth and authenticity to the novel's dark and suspenseful atmosphere.

- In *The Lincoln Lawyer* by Michael Connelly, defense attorney Mickey Haller navigates the streets of Los Angeles, California, as he defends a wealthy client accused of murder. The Urban Jungle setting of Los Angeles depicts the city as a sprawling metropolis teeming with crime, corruption, and intrigue, providing a vivid backdrop for the novel's gripping courtroom drama and street-level action.

- In *The City & The City* by China Miéville, Inspector Tyador Borlú investigates a murder that blurs the boundaries between two overlapping cities—Besźel and Ul Qoma. The Urban Jungle trope explores the intricacies and tensions of urban life, as Borlú navigates the complex social, cultural, and political dynamics of these intertwined cities while unraveling the mystery at their heart.

The Urban Jungle trope continues to be a dynamic and captivating element of mystery fiction, offering authors a diverse array of settings and characters to explore within the bustling metropolises of the world. This trope demonstrates the enduring appeal of the city setting in captivating readers with tales of crime, justice, and the human condition.

CHAPTER 7

Genre Tropes for the Mystery Genre

enre tropes are recurring themes, motifs, or elements commonly found within specific genres of literature, film, and other forms of media. These tropes serve as familiar conventions or storytelling devices audiences associate with particular genres, such as mystery, romance, science fiction, fantasy, and more. While some may view tropes as clichés to be avoided, they can actually be powerful tools for enhancing storytelling and connecting with audiences.

One key benefit of genre tropes is their ability to establish and reinforce genre expectations. For example, in the mystery genre, readers anticipate elements like a puzzling crime, a determined detective, and a satisfying resolution. By incorporating these tropes into their stories, writers can signal to readers what type of narrative experience they can expect and create a sense of familiarity and comfort. This familiarity can be particularly appealing to fans of specific genres who enjoy the conventions and formulas that define them.

Additionally, genre tropes can provide a framework for storytelling and serve as a source of inspiration for writers. Rather than starting from scratch, writers can draw upon established tropes within their chosen genre to structure their plots, develop characters, and craft compelling narratives. For example, the "chosen one" trope often found in fantasy literature can inspire writers to create protagonists who embark on epic quests and fulfill destinies that transcend ordinary life. By leveraging familiar tropes, writers can streamline the creative process and focus on refining their ideas within the established parameters of their chosen genre.

Genre tropes can facilitate genre blending and experimentation, allowing writers to subvert or reinvent familiar conventions to create fresh and innovative stories. For example, a writer may incorporate elements of romance into a science fiction narrative or blend elements of horror with historical fiction. By combining tropes from different genres, writers can create unique and compelling narratives that appeal to a wider range of readers and defy traditional genre boundaries. This flexibility encourages creativity and exploration, enabling writers to push the boundaries of genre fiction and explore new storytelling possibilities.

Forensic Evidence Trope
(FM, LT, PP)

Forensic Evidence Trope Overview

The Forensic Evidence trope is a staple in mystery and crime fiction, featuring the use of scientific methods and analysis to solve criminal cases. Forensic evidence encompasses a wide range of techniques, including DNA analysis, fingerprinting, ballistics, and toxicology, among others. These methods are employed by law enforcement professionals and forensic experts to gather clues, identify suspects, and build a case against perpetrators. In many stories, the meticulous examination of forensic evidence plays a pivotal role in unraveling complex mysteries and uncovering the truth behind crimes. The inclusion of forensic elements adds authenticity and realism to the narrative, as well as highlighting the importance of science in modern criminal investigations. Additionally, the portrayal of forensic procedures often lends a sense of procedural detail and intrigue to mystery plots, captivating readers with the intricacies of crime-solving techniques.

The Forensic Evidence trope is commonly found in various mystery sub-genres, where it plays a significant role in unraveling the intricacies of the plot and solving crimes. One of the primary sub-genres where this trope is prevalent is the police procedural mystery. In these narratives, forensic evidence, such as DNA analysis, fingerprinting, ballistics, and autopsy reports, is often central to the investigation process conducted by law enforcement agencies. Through meticulous examination and analysis of forensic clues, detectives piece together crucial details that lead to the apprehension of suspects and the resolution of the case.

Obviously, the sub-genre where the Forensic Evidence trope frequently appears is the sub-genre it created—the forensic mystery itself. In these stories, forensic scientists, medical examiners, or crime scene investigators take center stage as protagonists, utilizing their specialized knowledge and expertise to solve crimes. These narratives often delve deep into the intricacies of forensic science, exploring various techniques and technologies used to analyze evidence and uncover hidden truths. The meticulous examination of forensic evidence serves as a driving force behind the narrative's progression, leading to compelling plot twists and revelations.

The Forensic Evidence trope is prevalent in legal thriller mysteries, where forensic findings play a crucial role in courtroom proceedings and the pursuit of justice. Lawyers and prosecutors leverage forensic evidence to build their cases, presenting scientific findings as irrefutable proof of guilt or innocence. These narratives often explore the intersection of law and science, highlighting the importance of forensic expertise in the legal system. The presentation and interpretation of forensic evidence during trials add layers of tension and intrigue to the storyline, keeping readers engaged as they await the outcome of the legal proceedings.

Across these narratives, forensic evidence serves as a powerful tool wielded by investigators, forensic scientists, and legal professionals to uncover truths, solve crimes, and deliver justice. Its presence adds depth and authenticity to the storytelling, offering readers a glimpse into the fascinating world of forensic science and its pivotal role in unraveling mysteries.

Why Readers Love the Forensic Evidence Trope

The Forensic Evidence trope is a reader favorite for several reasons. First, the use of forensic science adds an element of realism and authenticity to the narrative. As readers immerse themselves in the story, they appreciate the meticulous attention to detail and the accuracy of forensic procedures depicted in the investigation process. This realism enhances the overall credibility of the plot and allows readers to feel more deeply engaged in the story's progression.

The Forensic Evidence trope also offers a unique and intellectually stimulating aspect to mystery novels. Readers are fascinated by the intricacies of forensic science, from analyzing blood spatter patterns to deciphering complex DNA evidence. The portrayal of forensic techniques and technologies provides readers with an opportunity to learn about the scientific methods used in real-life criminal investigations, satisfying their curiosity and thirst for knowledge.

Of course, the Forensic Evidence trope also often introduces a sense of suspense and intrigue to the storyline. As forensic clues are uncovered and analyzed, readers eagerly anticipate the revelation of crucial evidence that could turn the investigation in new and unexpected directions. The gradual accumulation of forensic evidence builds tension throughout the narrative, keeping readers gripped with the unfolding drama as they speculate about the identity of the culprit and the resolution of the mystery.

When used effectively, the Forensic Evidence trope allows for the exploration of complex moral and ethical dilemmas. As forensic scientists and investigators grapple with the implications of their findings, readers are presented with thought-provoking questions about the nature of justice, the reliability of scientific evidence, and the consequences of forensic mistakes. This adds depth and nuance to the narrative, prompting readers to reflect on the broader societal issues raised by the use of forensic evidence in criminal investigations.

What to Watch for When Using the Forensic Evidence Trope

When utilizing the Forensic Evidence trope in your novels, be mindful of the following pitfalls to be sure it's effective and realistic portrayal.

1. **Accuracy of Depiction:** Conduct thorough research to accurately represent forensic procedures and techniques. Inaccurate or unrealistic portrayals of forensic science can undermine the credibility of the narrative and lead to reader disengagement. This is crucial to successfully using this trope.

2. **Balancing Realism with Storytelling:** While realism is important, it's important to also balance the technical aspects of forensic science with the need to maintain narrative pacing and reader interest. Avoid overwhelming readers with excessive technical details that detract from the flow of the story.

3. **Ethical Considerations:** Consider the ethical implications of using forensic evidence in your narratives. Avoid glorifying or sensationalizing forensic procedures and be mindful of the

potential impact on real-world perceptions of forensic science and criminal justice.

4. **Maintaining Suspense without Sacrificing Realism:** While forensic evidence can contribute to the suspense of a mystery novel, be sure the use of your forensic techniques aligns with real-world limitations and constraints. Avoid relying on overly convenient or contrived forensic breakthroughs to resolve the plot.

Approach the use of the Forensic Evidence trope in your novels with careful consideration and attention to detail. This will help you leverage forensic evidence to enhance your mystery narratives.

Examples of the Forensic Evidence Trope

The Forensic Evidence trope is a cornerstone of mystery fiction, allowing investigators to employ scientific methods to solve crimes and uncover the truth. From DNA analysis to fingerprinting, forensic evidence adds a layer of authenticity and intrigue to the investigative process, often leading to unexpected twists and revelations. Following are examples of mystery genre books that skillfully utilize the Forensic Evidence trope to immerse readers in thrilling tales of investigation and deduction.

- In *The Bone Collector* by Jeffery Deaver, quadriplegic forensic detective Lincoln Rhyme and his partner Amelia Sachs track down a sadistic serial killer terrorizing New York City. The author uses the Forensic Evidence trope by showcasing Rhyme's meticulous analysis of physical evidence, from bone fragments to trace fibers, as he races against time to catch the elusive murderer.

- Dr. Kay Scarpetta, a forensic pathologist, investigates a series of brutal murders in Richmond, Virginia, in *Postmortem* by Patricia Cornwell. She uses cutting-edge forensic techniques to identify the killer. The Forensic Evidence trope immerses readers in Scarpetta's world of autopsies, DNA analysis, and crime scene reconstruction, as she pieces together the clues that will lead her to the truth.

- In *The Silence of the Lambs* by Thomas Harris, FBI trainee Clarice Starling seeks the help of incarcerated serial killer Hannibal Lecter to catch another murderer known as Buffalo Bill. Starling uses forensic psychology and behavioral analysis to understand the motivations and methods of the killers, adding depth and complexity to the investigation.

The Forensic Evidence trope remains a vital and compelling element of mystery fiction, allowing authors to weave intricate narratives of crime and detection using the latest advancements in forensic science. Whether it's the meticulous analysis of physical evidence or the psychological profiling of suspects, these books demonstrate the enduring appeal of the Forensic Evidence trope in captivating readers with tales of investigation, deduction, and justice.

Legal Proceedings Trope
(LT, PP)

Legal Proceedings Trope Overview

The Legal Proceedings trope is a narrative device frequently utilized in mystery and thriller genres, involving legal procedures and courtroom drama as central elements of the plot. In stories featuring this trope, the protagonist, often a lawyer, investigator, or defendant, becomes embroiled in a complex web of legal intricacies, including trials, hearings, depositions, and investigations. These legal proceedings serve as a backdrop for uncovering clues, presenting evidence, and unraveling the truth behind the mystery at hand. As the narrative unfolds, tension mounts as characters navigate the nuances of the legal system, grapple with moral dilemmas, and face off against cunning adversaries—be they rival attorneys, corrupt officials, or elusive criminals. The Legal Proceedings trope offers readers a compelling blend of suspense, intrigue, and intellectual challenge, as they follow the twists and turns of legal battles while eagerly anticipating the ultimate resolution of the case.

The Legal Proceedings trope is a common feature in various mystery sub-genres. The most prominent mystery sub-genre where the Legal Proceedings trope is prevalent is the associated legal thriller. In these stories, legal professionals often find themselves embroiled in high-stakes cases involving murder, corruption, or other crimes. The narrative typically revolves around courtroom battles, legal maneuvering, and the pursuit of justice, with protagonists using their legal acumen to uncover the truth and bring perpetrators to account.

Why Readers Love the Legal Proceedings Trope

Readers are drawn to the Legal Proceedings trope in mystery novels for several compelling reasons. The legal setting adds an extra layer of complexity and realism to the story. Courtroom dramas and legal thrillers often present intricate legal procedures, debates, and strategies that mirror real-life courtroom proceedings. This authenticity can be highly engaging for readers who enjoy delving into the intricacies of the legal system and witnessing the battle of wits between opposing legal teams.

Moreover, the Legal Proceedings trope provides a fertile ground for suspense and tension to flourish. Courtroom scenes are inherently dramatic, with high stakes, intense cross-examinations, and unexpected revelations keeping readers on the edge of anticipation. The unfolding of a trial, with its twists and turns, can captivate readers as they eagerly anticipate the outcome and speculate about the guilt or innocence of the accused.

This trope often explores complex moral and ethical dilemmas that ring true with readers. Legal thrillers, in particular, may delve into themes such as justice, morality, and the gray areas of the law, prompting readers to ponder questions of right and wrong. Characters grappling with ethical quandaries and facing tough decisions can add depth to the narrative, fostering empathy and emotional investment from readers who are eager to see how these dilemmas are resolved.

It offers a fascinating glimpse into the workings of the legal profession and the roles of lawyers, judges, and other legal professionals. Readers may be intrigued by the strategies employed by attorneys, the tactics used during cross-examination, and the nuances of courtroom etiquette. This insider perspective can be both educational and entertaining, allowing readers to gain insights into the legal world while immersing themselves in a gripping mystery narrative.

What to Watch for When Using the Legal Proceedings Trope

When incorporating the Legal Proceedings trope into your novels, be mindful of the following items to get the most out of this trope.

1. **Lack of Research:** Conduct thorough research into legal procedures, courtroom etiquette, and the workings of the legal system to guarantee accuracy and authenticity in your portrayal. Failing to do so can lead to inaccuracies or unrealistic depictions that may undermine the credibility of the story.

2. **Overuse of Legal Jargon:** While legal terminology adds authenticity to the narrative, excessive use of complex jargon can alienate readers who are unfamiliar with legal terms. Strive to strike a balance between authenticity and accessibility, ensuring legal terminology is used judiciously and explained when necessary.

3. **Predictability:** Legal proceedings can become formulaic if the plot follows clichéd tropes or predictable courtroom drama scenarios. Strive to inject fresh perspectives, unexpected twists,

and unique challenges into the legal aspects of the story to keep readers engaged and guessing.

4. **Unrealistic Dramatization:** While courtroom scenes are inherently dramatic, avoid overdramatizing or sensationalizing legal proceedings to the point of implausibility. Excessive melodrama or exaggerated courtroom theatrics can strain credibility and diminish the impact of pivotal moments in the story.

5. **Neglecting Character Development:** In the midst of legal maneuverings and courtroom drama, you may overlook the importance of character development. It's essential to flesh out the personalities, motivations, and internal conflicts of legal professionals and other characters involved in the proceedings to create depth and emotional resonance.

While the Legal Proceedings trope offers rich storytelling potential, you must navigate potential pitfalls to ensure your portrayal of legal proceedings is compelling, authentic, and engaging for readers. By conducting thorough research, striking a balance between authenticity and accessibility, avoiding predictability, maintaining realism, and prioritizing character development, you can effectively leverage the Legal Proceedings trope to enhance your mystery narratives.

Examples of the Legal Proceedings Trope

The Legal Proceedings trope adds layers of complexity and drama to the narrative as characters navigate the intricacies of the legal system. From courtroom battles to behind-the-scenes investigations. These stories explore themes of justice, truth, and the human condition. Following are examples of mystery genre books that skillfully incorporate the Legal Proceedings trope to immerse readers in gripping tales of crime, punishment, and redemption.

- In the classic novel, *To Kill a Mockingbird* by Harper Lee, lawyer Atticus Finch defends a black man falsely accused of raping a white woman in the racially-charged atmosphere of 1930s Alabama. The Legal Proceedings trope is central to the novel's exploration of prejudice and injustice, as Atticus fights for his client's innocence in the face of overwhelming social and legal opposition.

- In *Presumed Innocent* by Scott Turow, prosecuting attorney Rusty Sabich finds himself accused of murder, forcing him to navigate the treacherous waters of the criminal justice system while uncovering shocking secrets about his colleagues and friends. The Legal Proceedings trope is used to full effect in this gripping courtroom drama, as Rusty's trial becomes a battleground where truth and lies collide, leading to a stunning climax that keeps readers guessing until the very end.

- Assistant District Attorney Andy Barber finds himself torn between his duty to uphold the law and his love for his son, who is accused of a brutal murder, in *Defending Jacob* by William Landay. The Legal Proceedings trope is used to explore themes of family loyalty and moral ambiguity as Andy grapples with the implications of his son's innocence or guilt, leading to a gripping courtroom showdown that challenges everything he thought he knew.

The Legal Proceedings trope offers authors a rich tapestry of characters, conflicts, and moral dilemmas to explore within the context of the legal system. Whether it's the pursuit of justice in the face of prejudice or the battle for truth in a world of lies, these books demonstrate the use of the Legal Proceedings trope in captivating readers with tales of crime, punishment, and the quest for redemption.

Noir Fiction Trope
(HBM, NM, PT)

Noir Fiction Trope Overview

The Noir Fiction trope encapsulates a gritty and atmospheric style of storytelling deeply rooted in crime, cynicism, and moral ambiguity. Originating in the early 20th century, particularly in hard-boiled detective novels and film noir cinema, this trope paints a bleak and shadowy portrayal of urban landscapes and human nature. Characters often navigate through seedy underworlds, filled with corruption, betrayal, and existential despair, as they grapple with their own moral compromises and dark pasts. Themes of alienation, disillusionment, and fatalism pervade noir narratives, characterized by morally ambiguous protagonists, femme fatales, and morally bankrupt antagonists. Visual elements such as stark lighting, moody cinematography, and chiaroscuro imagery enhance the noir atmosphere, evoking a sense of foreboding and unease. Despite its bleak outlook, noir fiction captivates audiences with its immersive atmosphere, complex characters, and intricate plots, offering a compelling exploration of the human condition amidst the shadows of society.

The Noir Fiction trope is most commonly found in various mystery sub-genres that explore the darker aspects of human nature and society. One of the primary sub-genres where Noir Fiction thrives is hard-boiled mystery. Originating in the pulp fiction era of the early 20th century, hard-boiled mystery features gritty, cynical protagonists navigating through a world rife with corruption, violence, and moral ambiguity. These stories often unfold in urban settings, where the seedy underbelly of society is laid bare, and protagonists operate on the fringes of the law to achieve their goals.

Of course, the mystery sub-genre most closely associated with Noir Fiction is the noir mystery sub-genre. In noir mystery, readers follow detectives or private investigators as they delve into complex cases involving murder, betrayal, and deception. These stories typically feature morally ambiguous characters, intricate plots, and atmospheric settings that conjours a sense of bleakness and despair. The protagonists often find themselves entangled in webs of deceit and danger, where the line between right and wrong is blurred, and justice is elusive.

Noir Fiction trope can be prevalent psychological thrillers too. In this sub-genre, protagonists grapple with their own inner demons while navigating treacherous external threats, leading to a deep exploration of the human psyche and motivations. This sub-genre often features morally ambiguous characters, intricate plotlines, and atmospheric settings that kindle the mood and tone of classic film noir.

Overall, the Noir Fiction trope finds a home in a diverse range of mystery sub-genres. Its enduring appeal lies in its ability to captivate readers with its exploration of the darker aspects of human nature, its morally ambiguous characters, and its atmospheric settings that rouse a sense of mystery, intrigue, and danger. Whether set in the gritty streets of a bustling metropolis or the shadowy corners of the human mind, Noir Fiction continues to enthrall readers with its compelling narratives and timeless themes.

Why Readers Love the Noir Fiction Trope

Readers are drawn to the Noir Fiction trope for its captivating portrayal of moral ambiguity and gritty realism. One reason for its popularity is its complex and flawed characters who navigate morally ambiguous situations. Unlike traditional heroes, protagonists in Noir Fiction often possess a dark past or questionable motivation, making them more relatable and intriguing to readers. This moral complexity adds depth to the story, as readers are compelled to explore the inner workings of these characters' minds and motivations.

The atmospheric settings and moody aesthetics of Noir Fiction create an immersive reading experience that hits home with audiences. Whether it's the dimly lit streets of a bustling city or the desolate landscapes of a remote town, these settings ellicit a sense of mystery, danger, and intrigue. The vivid descriptions and evocative imagery transport readers to a world where shadows conceal as much as they reveal, heightening the tension and suspense of the narrative.

Readers are drawn to Noir Fiction for its exploration of universal themes such as betrayal, corruption, and existential angst. Through the lens of crime and mystery, Noir Fiction delves into the darker aspects of human nature, offering thought-provoking insights into the human condition. The genre's focus on societal issues and moral dilemmas provides readers with a compelling framework for examining the complexities of life and the choices we make.

Ultimately, readers love Noir Fiction because it offers a captivating blend of suspense, intrigue, and psychological depth. Whether they're searching for thrilling plot twists, morally ambiguous characters, or atmospheric settings, Noir Fiction delivers a compelling reading experience that keeps them hooked from beginning to end. As a result, the genre continues to captivate audiences and remains a perennial favorite among mystery enthusiasts.

What to Watch for When Using the Noir Fiction Trope

Using the Noir Fiction trope in a novel can be enticing when you're seeking to create atmospheric, morally complex narratives. However, there are certain pitfalls you need to be wary of when using this storytelling device. Here are some considerations:

1. **Overly Clichéd Characters:** While flawed and morally ambiguous characters are a hallmark of Noir Fiction, relying too heavily on stereotypes can make characters feel one-dimensional and predictable. Strive to imbue your characters with depth and complexity to avoid falling into clichés.

2. **Contrived Plot Twists:** Noir Fiction often features unexpected plot twists and turns, but be cautious not to introduce twists solely for the sake of shock value. Plot twists should feel organic and arise naturally from the characters' motivations and the story's internal logic.

3. **Excessive Bleakness:** While Noir Fiction typically explores dark and gritty themes, an overly bleak tone can become overwhelming for readers. It's essential to balance darkness with moments of lightness, hope, or redemption to maintain engagement and prevent the narrative from feeling monotonous.

4. **Lack of Originality:** The Noir Fiction genre has a rich history and well-established conventions, but strive to bring fresh

perspectives and original ideas to your work. Rehashing tired tropes without adding anything new can lead to a derivative and uninspired story.

5. **Neglecting Atmosphere:** Atmosphere plays a crucial role in Noir Fiction, setting the mood and immersing readers in the story's world. Pay careful attention to creating evocative settings and sensory details to enhance the atmosphere and draw readers into the narrative.

While Noir Fiction offers a wealth of opportunities for crafting compelling and atmospheric stories, it's essential to approach the genre with caution. By avoiding clichés, maintaining narrative balance, and infusing your work with originality and atmosphere, you can effectively harness the power of the Noir Fiction trope to captivate readers and create memorable storytelling experiences.

Examples of the Noir Fiction Trope

Noir fiction is a distinct subgenre of mystery that delves into the gritty and morally ambiguous world of crime, corruption, and disillusionment. With its dark atmosphere, morally complex characters, and bleak urban settings, noir fiction captivates readers with its atmospheric storytelling and psychological depth. Let's look at some examples of the Noir Fiction trope as it immerses readers in gripping tales of intrigue, betrayal, and moral ambiguity.

- In *The Maltese Falco* by Dashiell Hammett, private detective Sam Spade becomes embroiled in a web of deception and murder when he is hired to track down a valuable statuette known as the

Maltese Falcon. The Noir Fiction trope is central to the novel's atmosphere, as Spade navigates the seedy underbelly of 1930s San Francisco, where everyone has a hidden agenda and nothing is as it seems.

- Private investigator Philip Marlowe is hired to investigate a case of blackmail and murder involving a wealthy family with dark secrets, in *The Big Sleep* by Raymond Chandler. The Noir Fiction trope is used to full effect in this gritty and atmospheric novel, as Marlowe delves into the corrupt and morally bankrupt world of 1940s Los Angeles, where the line between good and evil is blurred and justice is hard to come by.

- In *The Long Goodbye* by Raymond Chandler, Philip Marlowe is drawn into a tangled web of murder, deception, and betrayal when he becomes embroiled in the life of a troubled war veteran. The Noir Fiction trope is masterfully employed to explore themes of loneliness, alienation, and existential despair as Marlowe navigates the seedy streets of Los Angeles, where danger lurks around every corner and redemption seems elusive.

The Noir Fiction trope features gritty realism, morally complex characters, and bleak urban settings. Whether it's the seedy streets of 1930s San Francisco or the corrupt small towns of the American Midwest, these books captivate readers with tales of crime, betrayal, and moral ambiguity.

Police Procedural Trope
(FM, LT, PP, PT, SKM)

Police Procedural Trope Overview

The Police Procedural trope is a staple of mystery fiction, focusing on the investigative procedures and protocols followed by law enforcement agencies to solve crimes. These stories often center around police detectives or officers working within a department, task force, or precinct to investigate and apprehend criminals. The narrative typically follows a structured format, detailing the step-by-step process of solving a case, from the initial crime scene investigation to the arrest and prosecution of suspects. Police procedurals are known for their attention to detail and realism, often incorporating authentic police terminology, forensic science techniques, and legal procedures. Characters in police procedural stories range from seasoned detectives to rookie officers, each bringing their own skills, expertise, and personal baggage to the investigation. The genre offers readers a glimpse into the inner workings of law enforcement agencies, portraying the challenges, triumphs, and ethical dilemmas faced by those dedicated to upholding the law and seeking justice.

The Police Procedural trope is commonly found in several sub-genres that revolve around law enforcement and criminal investigation. One prominent sub-genre where the Police Procedural trope thrives is the sub-genre this trope spawned—the police procedural sub-genre. In this sub-genre, police officers are the central characters tasked with solving crimes. These stories often follow the step-by-step investigative process, showcasing the meticulous methods employed by law enforcement to unravel complex cases and bring perpetrators to justice. Of course, this trope isn't limited to just its self-named sub-genre.

The Police Procedural trope is also prevalent is legal thrillers, which focus on legal professionals such as prosecutors, defense attorneys, and law enforcement personnel navigating the intricacies of the legal system. In these stories, the police procedural element often plays a crucial role in gathering evidence, conducting interviews, and building a case against suspects or defendants, adding layers of authenticity and realism to the legal proceedings depicted. Additionally, the Police Procedural trope frequently appears in forensic mysteries, where forensic scientists, medical examiners, and crime scene investigators take center stage in solving crimes through the application of scientific methods and forensic techniques. These stories delve into the technical aspects of crime scene analysis, DNA testing, and ballistics examination, showcasing how law enforcement utilizes cutting-edge technology and forensic expertise to crack cases. It can also be found in serial killer thrillers and psychological thrillers, where detectives or profilers are tasked with hunting down elusive serial killers or unraveling the twisted motives behind psychopathic crimes. These stories often delve into the psyche of both the perpetrator and the investigator, exploring the psychological toll of chasing dangerous criminals and the moral dilemmas faced by law enforcement in their pursuit of justice.

Overall, the Police Procedural trope finds a home in various mystery sub-genres, adding authenticity, detail, and procedural accuracy to narratives centered around crime-solving and law enforcement investigation.

Whether it's through the lens of seasoned detectives, legal professionals, forensic experts, or psychological profilers, the portrayal of police procedures serves to immerse readers in the intricate world of criminal investigation and the pursuit of truth and justice.

Why Readers Love the Police Procedural Trope

Readers are drawn to the Police Procedural trope for several reasons. These stories offer a realistic and detailed portrayal of police work, providing insight into the investigative process and the inner workings of law enforcement agencies. The meticulous attention to detail and accuracy in depicting police procedures, forensic techniques, and legal protocols lend authenticity to the narratives, immersing readers in the world of crime-solving. This authenticity creates a sense of credibility and trustworthiness, making the plots more engaging and believable.

Police Procedural stories often feature complex and multifaceted characters, including detectives, forensic experts, and other members of law enforcement teams. These characters are typically well-developed and undergo personal growth and transformation throughout the course of the narrative. Readers become emotionally invested in their journeys, rooting for them as they navigate through challenging cases, confront moral dilemmas, and grapple with their own flaws and vulnerabilities. The human element adds depth and richness to the storytelling, eliciting empathy and connection from the audience.

Narratives with the Police Procedural trope often explore themes of justice, morality, and the complexities of the criminal justice system. These stories delve into the ethical dilemmas faced by law enforcement professionals, such as the balance between upholding the law and protecting individual rights, or the pursuit of justice in the face of institutional corruption or systemic injustice. By grappling with these weighty issues, Police Procedural novels offer readers not only thrilling mysteries but also thought-provoking insights into the human condition and society as a whole.

Overall, the Police Procedural trope appeals to readers who enjoy immersive and intellectually stimulating crime fiction. With its blend of meticulous research, compelling characters, and exploration of moral and ethical dilemmas, Police Procedural stories captivate audiences and keep them eagerly turning the pages until the very end.

What to Watch for When Using the Police Procedural Trope

When incorporating the Police Procedural trope into your novels, there are certain pitfalls that can detract from your storytelling, if you aren't mindful. Here are some key considerations to keep in mind:

1. **Accuracy and Authenticity:** It's essential to conduct thorough research to be certain of your accuracy in depicting police procedures, forensic techniques, and legal protocols. Inaccuracies or unrealistic portrayals can undermine the credibility of the narrative and break the reader's immersion in the story.

2. **Balancing Procedural Detail with Narrative Pace:** While readers appreciate the authenticity of procedural details, excessive focus on technicalities can slow down the pacing of the story and bog down the narrative. Strive to strike a balance between procedural accuracy and maintaining a brisk, compelling pace that keeps the story moving forward.

3. **Developing Complex Characters:** In Police Procedural novels, characters often play a central role in driving the story forward. Take care to develop multidimensional characters with depth, complexity, and relatability. Avoid relying on stereotypes or one-dimensional portrayals, and instead, invest time in fleshing out characters with distinct personalities, motivations, and arcs.

4. **Avoiding Overreliance on Forensic Science:** While forensic science can be a fascinating aspect of Police Procedural stories, be cautious not to overuse it as a narrative crutch. Remember forensic evidence is just one tool in the investigative process, and it's essential to maintain a balance between scientific analysis and traditional detective work.

Approaching the Police Procedural trope with careful attention to detail, originality, and character development is key. By prioritizing accuracy, avoiding clichés, balancing procedural detail with narrative pace, developing complex characters, and using forensic science judiciously, you can create compelling and authentic Police Procedural novels that connect with readers.

Examples of Police Procedural Trope

Police procedural novels offer readers an immersive glimpse into the meticulous and often gritty world of law enforcement. These stories follow detectives as they methodically investigate crimes, gather evidence, and interrogate suspects in their quest for justice. Here are a few examples of mystery genre books that expertly employ the Police Procedural trope to engage readers in gripping tales of crime and investigation.

- Quadriplegic detective Lincoln Rhyme and his partner Amelia Sachs track down a sadistic serial killer terrorizing New York City, in *The Bone Collecto*" by Jeffery Deaver. The novel employs the Police Procedural trope as Rhyme and Sachs meticulously analyze crime scenes, forensic evidence, and behavioral patterns to identify and apprehend the perpetrator.

- In *The Black Echo* by Michael Connelly, LAPD detective Harry Bosch investigates the murder of a fellow Vietnam War veteran, uncovering a web of corruption and betrayal. The Police Procedural trope is central to the novel as Bosch and his colleagues methodically follow leads, conduct surveillance, and navigate bureaucratic obstacles in their pursuit of justice.

- In *Still Life* by Louise Penny, Chief Inspector Armand Gamache of the Sûreté du Québec investigates the suspicious death of an elderly woman in the tranquil village of Three Pines. The Police Procedural trope is skillfully employed as Gamache and his team meticulously gather evidence, interview witnesses, and analyze motives to uncover the truth behind the seemingly idyllic facade of the small town.

Police procedural novels continue to captivate readers with their intricate plots, detailed investigative techniques, and compelling characters. Whether it's the mean streets of New York City or the tranquil villages of rural Quebec, these mystery genre books demonstrate the enduring appeal of the Police Procedural trope in engaging readers with tales of crime, investigation, and justice.

Supernatural Mystery Trope
(CM, GM, HM, OM, PM)

Supernatural Mystery Trope Overview

The Supernatural Mystery trope intertwines elements of the paranormal with traditional mystery narratives, blurring the lines between the natural and the supernatural. In these stories, protagonists investigate otherworldly occurrences, unexplained phenomena, and supernatural beings such as ghosts, vampires, or werewolves. The narrative often delves into ancient myths, folklore, and occult rituals, as characters confront dark forces beyond human comprehension. Supernatural detectives or investigators employ both rational deduction and supernatural abilities to unravel the mysteries, adding an extra layer of intrigue and suspense. Themes of fear, the unknown, and the existence of unseen realms are explored, creating an atmospheric and chilling backdrop for the unfolding mystery.

The Supernatural Mystery trope finds its home in various mystery sub-genres, each incorporating elements of the supernatural to add an extra layer of intrigue and mystique to the narrative. One prominent sub-genre where the Supernatural Mystery trope frequently appears is the paranormal mystery. In these stories, supernatural phenomena such as ghosts, hauntings, and psychic abilities play a central role in driving the plot forward and solving the mystery. Paranormal investigators or protagonists with supernatural powers often navigate the blurred lines between the natural and supernatural worlds to uncover the truth behind inexplicable occurrences.

Beyond its associated sub-genre, the Supernatural Mystery trope can sometimes be found in the historical mystery sub-genre, blending elements of the supernatural with historical settings and events. These stories transport readers to bygone eras where superstition, folklore, and mysticism intertwine with real-world historical events, providing a unique backdrop for solving mysteries steeped in both the mundane and the supernatural. Whether set in Victorian London, medieval Europe, or ancient civilizations, these narratives offer a captivating blend of history, mystery, and the supernatural.

Of course, one of the most popular applications of the Supernatural Mystery trope in today's market can be found in cozy mysteries. Quaint, picturesque settings serve as the backdrop for lighthearted mysteries infused with elements of the supernatural. This has become so prevalent, there is an ever-growing subset of this genre known as paranormal cozies.

The Supernatural Mystery trope transcends traditional genre boundaries, seamlessly weaving elements of the supernatural into various mystery sub-genres to create captivating narratives that blur the line between reality and the supernatural realm. Whether exploring haunted houses, delving into ancient myths, or navigating contemporary urban landscapes teeming with supernatural creatures, these stories offer readers a thrilling journey into the unknown, where mysteries wait to be unraveled amidst the shadows of the supernatural.

Why Readers Love the Supernatural Mystery Trope

Readers are drawn to the Supernatural Mystery trope for its ability to infuse storytelling with an added layer of intrigue, suspense, and escapism. One reason for its popularity is the sense of wonder and excitement it sparks. The inclusion of supernatural elements such as ghosts, magic, or mythical creatures adds an element of the unknown, sparking curiosity and inviting readers to explore worlds beyond the confines of reality. This sense of mystery and wonderment keeps readers engaged as they eagerly anticipate uncovering the secrets hidden within the supernatural realm.

Additionally, the Supernatural Mystery trope offers readers a unique blend of genres, combining elements of mystery with fantasy, horror, or paranormal fiction into their beloved mystery genre. This fusion creates a rich tapestry of storytelling possibilities, allowing authors to explore themes of the supernatural while delivering compelling mystery narratives. Readers are drawn to the genre-blurring nature of these stories, which often challenge conventions and offer fresh perspectives on traditional mystery tropes.

It appeals to readers' imaginations and sense of escapism. By immersing themselves in worlds where magic is real, ghosts roam the earth, and ancient curses hold sway, readers can temporarily escape the constraints of everyday life and embark on thrilling adventures in fantastical realms. The supernatural elements add an element of excitement and unpredictability, keeping readers gripped with suspense as they follow protagonists who navigate the supernatural landscape in search of truth and justice.

With this trope, it allows authors to explore complex themes and issues through allegory and metaphor. By using supernatural elements as symbolic representations of real-world phenomena, authors can address social, cultural, or existential themes in a compelling and thought-provoking manner. This deeper layer of storytelling adds richness and depth to the narrative, resonating with readers on a profound level and leaving a lasting impact long after the story has ended.

What to Watch for When Using the Supernatural Mystery Trope

The Supernatural Mystery trope offers a lot of exciting ways to create unique and exciting storylines. However, there are a few things you'll want to be mindful of as you craft your story. These include:

1. **Balancing Realism and Fantasy:** Maintaining a delicate balance between the supernatural and the real world is crucial. Ascertain supernatural elements are integrated seamlessly into the story's setting and plot, avoiding inconsistencies or unrealistic scenarios that may strain readers' suspension of disbelief.

2. **Maintaining Internal Logic:** In supernatural mysteries, it's essential to establish clear rules and boundaries for the supernatural elements present in the story. Adhere to these rules consistently throughout the narrative to maintain internal logic and prevent plot holes or inconsistencies from detracting from the story's credibility.

3. **Developing Multidimensional Characters:** While supernatural mysteries often focus on the supernatural elements of the plot, it's essential not to overlook character development. Craft multidimensional characters with realistic motivations, flaws, and

complexities to guarantee readers remain invested in their journey, regardless of the supernatural elements at play.

4. **Avoiding Deus Ex Machina:** Be cautious of using supernatural elements as a convenient solution to resolve plot conflicts or tie up loose ends. Introducing supernatural interventions at key moments without proper foreshadowing or buildup can feel contrived and diminish the impact of the story's resolution.

While the Supernatural Mystery trope offers exciting storytelling possibilities, you must navigate its intricacies carefully to guarantee a compelling and cohesive narrative. By avoiding clichés, balancing realism and fantasy, maintaining internal logic, developing multidimensional characters, and steering clear of Deus Ex Machina, you can harness the power of the supernatural to create captivating mysteries that resonate with readers.

Examples of the Supernatural Mystery Trope

The Supernatural Mystery trope adds an extra layer of intrigue and suspense by incorporating elements of the paranormal into traditional detective stories. From ghosts and witches to curses and haunted houses, these novels blend the supernatural with mystery to create gripping and often chilling narratives. Here are a few examples of mystery genre books that utilize the Supernatural Mystery trope to thrill readers with tales of the unknown and the unexplained.

- In *The Hound of the Baskervilles* by Arthur Conan Doyle, Sherlock Holmes and Dr. John Watson investigate the mysterious death of Sir Charles Baskerville, rumored to be the result of a curse placed on his family by a spectral hound. The Supernatural Mystery trope is used to create an atmosphere of dread and uncertainty as Holmes and Watson confront the possibility of a supernatural explanation for the murders, ultimately unraveling the truth behind the legend.

- A group of people are invited to spend a summer in the notoriously haunted Hill House to investigate its supernatural phenomena, in *The Haunting of Hill House* by Shirley Jackson. The Supernatural Mystery trope is central to the novel as the characters grapple with the eerie occurrences and malevolent forces at play within the house, blurring the line between reality and the supernatural.

- In *The Woman in White* by Wilkie Collins, a mysterious woman dressed in white appears to Walter Hartright one night, setting off a chain of events that lead to murder, deception, and madness. The Supernatural Mystery trope is subtly woven into the novel's intricate plot, with elements of the supernatural serving as both red herrings and catalysts for the unfolding mystery.

The Supernatural Mystery trope offers readers an escape into worlds where the paranormal intersects with the mundane, creating thrilling and often chilling tales of mystery and intrigue. The Supernatural Mystery trope captivates readers with stories of the unknown and the unexplained.

Whodunit
(CM, FM, HBM, PP, PT, SKM, W)

The Whodunit trope is a classic mystery storytelling device where the central focus of the narrative revolves around solving a crime, usually a murder. In these stories, the primary question that drives the plot is "who committed the crime?" rather than "how" or "why." The protagonist, often a detective or amateur sleuth, works to uncover clues, interview suspects, and piece together evidence in order to identify the perpetrator. The tension in whodunit mysteries comes from the gradual unraveling of the mystery, as red herrings and false leads confound both the characters and the readers. Ultimately, the resolution of the mystery typically comes in the form of a dramatic reveal, where the identity of the culprit is unveiled, often accompanied by a surprising twist or revelation. Whodunit mysteries appeal to readers who enjoy unraveling puzzles and testing their deductive skills as they try to solve the mystery alongside the protagonist.

Whodunit stories often feature a closed-circle setting, such as a country estate or a locked room, where a group of suspects is confined, heightening the sense of tension and suspicion among the characters. The resolution of the mystery typically involves a dramatic revelation, where the detective unmasks the culprit and explains how the crime was committed, tying up loose ends and providing a satisfying conclusion for the reader.

The Whodunit trope is commonly found across various sub-genres within the mystery genre. In traditional whodunit sub-genre murder mysteries, the primary focus is on solving a murder case, often involving a detective or amateur sleuth who must uncover the identity of the perpetrator ("whodunit"). These stories typically feature clues, red herrings, and plot twists leading to the revelation of the culprit. Beyond the whodunit sub-genre, the Whodunit trope is often found in several other mystery sub-genres.

Despite their quaint settings, cozy mysteries often involve murder investigations where the central question is "whodunit." The emphasis is on puzzle-solving rather than graphic violence or suspense uses the Whodunit trope. In police procedural mysteries, the focus is on the investigative procedures and techniques used by law enforcement agencies to solve crimes. While these stories may involve complex investigations and multiple suspects, the ultimate goal is to uncover the identity of the perpetrator through systematic investigation, leading to the resolution of the "whodunit" question. Despite the focus on the detective's personal journey and moral ambiguity, in hard-boiled mysteries, these stories often center around solving mysteries and uncovering the truth behind crimes, including identifying the perpetrator in a "whodunit" scenario. And psychological thrillers often incorporate elements of mystery and suspense, with intricate plots and complex characters. In these stories, the identity of the perpetrator is frequently shrouded in ambiguity, leading to psychological tension and suspense as the protagonist attempts to unravel the mystery and determine "whodunit."

Overall, the Whodunit trope serves as a foundation for many mystery narratives, offering a framework for crafting engaging and suspenseful stories that challenge readers to unravel complex puzzles and uncover hidden truths. It capitalizes on the innate human curiosity about solving mysteries and provides a compelling narrative structure that keeps audiences hooked from beginning to end.

Why Readers Love the Whodunit Trope

Readers love the Whodunit trope for several reasons. It engages their analytical minds by presenting a puzzle to solve. The mystery surrounding the identity of the perpetrator creates suspense and anticipation, encouraging readers to actively participate in piecing together clues and unraveling the truth alongside the protagonist. This interactive aspect of the trope fosters a sense of immersion and intellectual challenge, making the reading experience more dynamic and rewarding.

The Whodunit trope taps into our innate curiosity about human behavior and motivations. As readers delve into the intricacies of the mystery, they are drawn into a web of deceit, intrigue, and hidden agendas. The gradual unveiling of clues, red herrings, and character motives adds layers of complexity to the narrative, keeping readers guessing and eager to uncover the truth behind the crime. This element of psychological suspense allows readers to explore the darker aspects of human nature from a safe distance, satisfying their fascination with the enigmatic workings of the human mind.

This trope offers a sense of closure and resolution that is deeply satisfying to readers. As the story unfolds and suspects are interrogated, readers are invested in the outcome, hoping for justice to prevail and the perpetrator to be unmasked. The moment of revelation, when the true identity of the culprit is finally revealed, delivers a powerful emotional payoff, validating the reader's efforts and investment in solving the mystery. This cathartic moment of clarity and closure not only fulfills the reader's desire for resolution but also provides a sense of narrative satisfaction that lingers long after the final page is turned.

Ultimately, the enduring appeal of the Whodunit trope lies in its ability to captivate and entertain readers with its blend of intellectual challenge, psychological depth, and narrative suspense. By inviting readers to become amateur sleuths and join the protagonist on a journey of discovery, the trope fosters a deeply immersive and engaging reading experience that transcends the boundaries of the page. Whether through classic murder mysteries or modern psychological thrillers, the Whodunit trope continues to captivate audiences with its timeless allure and universal appeal.

What to Watch for When Using the Whodunit Trope

Using the Whodunit trope in a novel can be a thrilling component of your writing, but you must tread carefully to ensure its effective execution without it feeling tired and overused. Here are some key considerations to keep in mind:

1. **Clarity of Clues:** Be sure the clues presented throughout the narrative are clear, logical, and consistent. Ambiguity or inconsistency in the clues can confuse readers and detract from the overall satisfaction of solving the mystery. Remember the reader only knows what you tell them.

2. **Use Beta Readers:** To guarantee your clues are clear, use beta readers and specifically ask them which clues they saw in your

novel. If your betas aren't finding clues you thought would be found by your readers, even after they've completed their reading and can look back with the benefit of hindsight, rewrite to bring them further to light.

3. **Avoiding Clichés:** While certain conventions of the Whodunit genre are expected, relying too heavily on clichés can make the story predictable and stale. Strive to inject originality and creativity into the plot and characterizations to keep readers engaged and guessing.

4. **Character Development:** Be mindful of developing well-rounded and believable characters, including both suspects and the protagonist. Each suspect should have plausible motives and a distinct personality, providing depth and complexity to the mystery.

5. **Pacing:** Pay attention to the pacing of the narrative, balancing moments of tension and revelation with periods of introspection and character development. Avoid rushing the resolution or prolonging the mystery beyond its natural conclusion, as this can lead to reader frustration or disinterest.

While the Whodunit trope offers endless opportunities for intrigue and suspense, approach its use with care and attention to detail. By crafting a well-structured plot, developing compelling characters, and skillfully deploying clues and red herrings, you can create a captivating mystery that keeps readers guessing until the very end.

Examples of the Whodunit Trope

The Whodunit trope is a classic element of mystery fiction, captivating readers with its intricate plots and tantalizing puzzles. In these stories, readers are invited to play detective alongside the characters as they unravel the clues, follow red herrings, and ultimately uncover the identity of the culprit. Here are some examples:

- When a passenger is murdered aboard the luxurious Orient Express train, detective Hercule Poirot must unravel the tangled web of secrets and lies to identify the killer, in *Murder on the Orient Express* by Agatha Christie. The Whodunit trope is central to the novel as Poirot meticulously interviews the passengers, scrutinizes their alibis, and uncovers hidden motives, leading to a shocking revelation that leaves readers stunned.

- In Agatha Christie's *The Mysterious Affair at Styles* her debut novel, Christie introduces readers to the iconic detective Hercule Poirot as he investigates a murder at an English country estate. The Whodunit trope is skillfully employed as Poirot sifts through a cast of eccentric characters, each with their own motives and secrets, to uncover the truth behind the murder and unmask the culprit.

- Private investigator Cormoran Strike is hired to investigate the apparent suicide of a supermodel, but soon discovers there may be more to the case than meets the eye, in *The Cuckoo's Calling* by Robert Galbraith (pseudonym for J.K. Rowling). The Whodunit trope drives the novel's plot as Strike meticulously sifts through a cast of suspects, each with their own motives and secrets, to uncover the truth behind the model's death.

The Whodunit trope tantalizes the readers with mysteries and clever plot twists, keeping them guessing until the very end. These books demonstrate the enduring appeal of the Whodunit trope in captivating readers with tales of intrigue, suspense, and the quest for truth.

CHAPTER 8

Plot Device Tropes for the Mystery Genre

Plot device tropes are narrative elements or mechanisms used by writers to advance the plot, create tension, develop characters, or resolve conflicts within a story. These tropes serve as tools writers can employ to structure their narratives and engage readers. While some plot device tropes may be familiar or even clichéd, when used effectively, they can add depth, complexity, and intrigue to a story.

One of the primary values of plot device tropes lies in their ability to drive the narrative forward and maintain reader interest. By introducing unexpected twists, dramatic revelations, or clever resolutions, plot device tropes can keep readers engaged and eager to discover what happens next. Additionally, these tropes can help writers navigate the complexities of storytelling by providing a framework for organizing plot elements and orchestrating key events.

Plot device tropes also offer writers opportunities to explore themes, motifs, and character dynamics in their stories. Whether it's a well-executed plot twist that challenges readers' assumptions, a cleverly devised MacGuffin that propels the protagonist on a quest, or a dramatic confrontation that reveals hidden truths, plot device tropes can deepen the thematic resonance of a narrative and enhance its emotional impact.

Furthermore, plot device tropes can serve as creative catalysts for writers, inspiring innovative ideas and sparking new directions for their stories. While some tropes may be conventional or formulaic, writers have the freedom to subvert expectations, reinvent familiar conventions, or combine multiple tropes in unique ways to craft original and compelling narratives.

These tropes are valuable tools writers can leverage to structure their stories, engage readers, explore themes, and ignite their creativity. When used judiciously and thoughtfully, plot device tropes can enrich storytelling, captivate audiences, and elevate the overall quality of a narrative.

Art Theft Trope
(CM, HCM, HM)

Art Theft Trope Overview

The Art Theft trope revolves around the stealing or illicit acquisition of valuable artworks, often serving as the central plot device in mystery, thriller, or heist narratives. Whether it's a daring museum heist, a sophisticated forgery scheme, or a clandestine auction of stolen masterpieces, the theft of art pieces sets the stage for intrigue, suspense, and high-stakes action. This trope frequently involves skilled thieves, cunning detectives, or art experts who navigate a world of deception, betrayal, and hidden agendas to recover the stolen treasures. The pursuit of justice may lead protagonists across continents, into the shadowy underworld of art crime, and even into conflict with powerful individuals or organizations seeking to profit from the illicit trade. The resolution of the art theft mystery often involves unexpected twists, intricate schemes, and revelations that shed light on the true motivations behind the crime, as well as the complex nature of art itself.

One sub-genre where the Art Theft trope frequently appears is the heist and caper mysteries sub-genre. In these stories, art often serves as both the subject of the mystery and a catalyst for the plot, often involving theft, forgery, or the illicit trade of valuable artworks. The protagonists, whether detectives, thieves, or art experts, navigate a world where art holds significant cultural and financial value, leading to high-stakes conflicts and complex investigations.

Another sub-genre where the Art Theft trope is prominent is the historical mystery sub-genre. In these stories, art may serve as a window into the past, providing clues to long-buried secrets or unsolved mysteries. Artifacts, paintings, or sculptures from different eras can hold hidden meanings or connections to historical events, prompting characters to delve into the past in search of answers. The blending of art and history adds layers of richness to the narrative, inviting readers to explore the intersections between artistry, culture, and intrigue.

Additionally, the Art Theft trope can be sometimes found in the cozy mystery sub-genre, albeit in a lighter and more whimsical context. In cozy mysteries, art-themed settings such as art galleries, museums, or artist colonies provide colorful backdrops for the unfolding mysteries. Art serves as a backdrop for the cozy community, with amateur sleuths often stumbling upon clues while attending art classes, exhibitions, or social events. The Art trope in cozy mysteries adds a touch of elegance and sophistication to the cozy world, offering readers a delightful escape into the realm of creativity and imagination.

The Art Theft trope's presence adds depth, intrigue, and cultural richness to narratives, inviting readers on captivating journeys through the worlds of art and mystery.

Why Readers Love the Art Theft Trope

Art possesses an inherent allure and mystique that captivates the imagination of readers. The world of art is often associated with beauty, creativity, and cultural significance, making it an intriguing backdrop for mysteries. Whether it's a priceless masterpiece or a mysterious artifact, art items hold a sense of mystery and intrigue, inviting readers to uncover their secrets alongside the characters.

The Art Theft trope offers a unique lens through which to explore complex themes and human emotions. Art has the power to evoke strong reactions and emotions, from admiration and awe to jealousy and greed. In mysteries, the discovery, theft, or forgery of art pieces can serve as a catalyst for the plot, highlighting themes of obsession, betrayal, and redemption. The interplay between characters and art objects adds layers of depth and complexity to the narrative, engaging readers on both intellectual and emotional levels.

It often introduces readers to fascinating worlds and subcultures they may not be familiar with. Whether it's the cutthroat world of high-end art auctions, the meticulous craftsmanship of forgers, or the vibrant community of street artists, art-themed mysteries offer glimpses into diverse and vibrant settings. Readers are transported to exotic locales, historical periods, or hidden corners of society, enriching their reading experience with new sights, sounds, and sensations.

This trope provides an opportunity for readers to engage with puzzles and riddles in a unique and visually stimulating way. Mysteries involving art often feature cryptic clues, hidden messages, and elaborate schemes that challenge readers to piece together the puzzle alongside the characters. The thrill of unraveling a mystery, deciphering clues, and uncovering the truth keeps readers hooked from beginning to end, making the Art trope a perennial favorite in the world of mystery fiction.

When incorporating the Art Theft trope into your novels, there are a few things you need to consider. These include:

1. **Accuracy and Research:** Conduct thorough research into the art world, including art history, terminology, and industry practices. Factual inaccuracies can undermine the credibility of the story and distract readers who are knowledgeable about the subject matter.

2. **Balancing Detail with Pace:** While it's essential to provide enough detail to immerse readers in the world of art, maintain a brisk pace and avoid bogging down the narrative with excessive exposition. Strike a balance between descriptive passages and forward momentum to keep the story moving.

3. **Ethical Considerations:** Be sensitive to ethical issues surrounding the art world, such as cultural appropriation, the illicit trade of stolen artifacts, and the exploitation of artists. Avoid glorifying criminal behavior or romanticizing unethical practices, and strive to present a nuanced portrayal of the characters' motivations and actions.

4. **Avoiding Stereotypes:** Be cautious of falling into stereotypes or clichéd portrayals of artists, collectors, or other characters associated with the art world. Instead, strive to create well-rounded and multidimensional characters with their own unique personalities, motivations, and flaws.

In conclusion, by approaching the Art trope with diligence, creativity, and sensitivity, you can craft compelling and authentic narratives that strike a chord with readers. With careful attention to detail, thoughtful research, and a willingness to explore new perspectives, the Art trope can enrich mystery novels and captivate audiences with its blend of intrigue, beauty, and suspense.

Examples of the Art Theft Trope

Art theft is a thrilling and captivating element of mystery fiction, often serving as the backdrop for tales of intrigue, deception, and high-stakes heists. From stolen masterpieces to elaborate forgeries, these stories immerse readers in the shadowy world of art crime, where nothing is as it seems and everyone has a hidden agenda. Here are some examples of the Art Theft trope in action:

- In *The Art Forger* by B.A. Shapiro, struggling artist Claire Roth is commissioned to forge a long-lost masterpiece by Degas, but soon finds herself embroiled in a web of deceit and betrayal. The Art Theft trope is central to the novel as Claire delves into the murky world of art forgery and theft, uncovering secrets that threaten to unravel the truth behind the painting's disappearance.

- FBI agent Kate O'Hare teams up with charming con artist Nick Fox to track down a stolen priceless artifact, leading them on a globe-trotting adventure filled with danger and double-crosses, in *The Heist* by Janet Evanovich and Lee Goldberg. The Art Theft trope drives the novel's plot as Kate and Nick race against time to recover the stolen treasure and outwit the mastermind behind the heist.

- In *The Last Painting of Sara de Vos* by Dominic Smith, the novel follows the intertwined stories of a 17th-century Dutch painting, its 20th-century owner, and a modern-day art historian. The Art Theft trope is skillfully woven throughout the novel as the characters grapple with questions of authenticity, ownership, and the true value of art, leading to a stunning revelation that ties together the threads of the past and the present.

Art theft continues to captivate readers with its thrilling and suspenseful tales of intrigue and deception. The Art Theft trope engages readers with stories of high-stakes adventure and the quest for justice.

Betrayal Trope
(HCM, NM, W)

Betrayal Trope Overview

The Betrayal trope is a powerful narrative device used across various genres, including mystery, drama, and fantasy, to introduce conflict and drama into a storyline. It revolves around the shocking revelation of deceit, disloyalty, or treachery perpetrated by one character against another, often a close friend, ally, or romantic partner. This trope can serve as a catalyst for character development, driving protagonists to reassess their relationships, values, and motivations in the face of betrayal. Betrayals can take many forms, from double-crosses and secret alliances to acts of sabotage and manipulation, adding layers of intrigue and complexity to the plot. Ultimately, the resolution of the betrayal trope often involves characters confronting the consequences of their actions, seeking redemption, or seeking revenge, leading to dramatic confrontations, emotional revelations, and unexpected twists in the narrative.

In traditional whodunit mysteries, betrayal often manifests as a character close to the protagonist—such as a friend, family member, or trusted ally—revealing themselves as the true culprit, betraying the protagonist's trust and complicating their investigation. Similarly, in psychological thrillers, betrayal may take the form of a protagonist's deteriorating mental state, leading them to question their own perceptions and motives as they uncover shocking truths about their past or the people around them.

In noir mysteries, the Betrayal trope is often central to the narrative, with morally ambiguous characters navigating a web of deceit and treachery in gritty, urban settings. The protagonist may find themselves betrayed by former partners, colleagues, or even romantic interests, highlighting the morally murky nature of their world. In legal thrillers, betrayal frequently occurs within the realm of professional ethics, as lawyers, judges, and law enforcement officials grapple with conflicting loyalties and hidden agendas that threaten to undermine the pursuit of justice.

Across all mystery sub-genres, the Betrayal trope serves to deepen character dynamics, heighten suspense, and keep readers guessing until the final reveal. Whether it's a shocking twist that upends everything the protagonist thought they knew or a slow-burning revelation that exposes long-held secrets, betrayal adds a compelling layer of tension and drama to mystery narratives, ensuring readers remain engaged and invested in the outcome.

Why Readers Love the Betrayal Trope

The Betrayal trope in mystery novels prompts powerful emotions and creates compelling storytelling dynamics that draws readers in. Betrayal taps into a universal human experience, resonating with readers on an emotional level as they empathize with characters who have been deceived or misled by those they trust. This emotional resonance adds depth to the narrative, making the stakes feel more personal and heightening the reader's investment in the outcome of the story.

It also introduces an element of suspense and unpredictability, keeping readers hanging on every word as they anticipate the next twist or revelation. The discovery of betrayal often serves as a turning point in the plot, propelling the protagonist into action and driving the story forward with newfound urgency. This narrative momentum creates a sense of momentum and tension that propels readers through the story, eager to uncover the truth behind the deception and see justice served.

The Betrayal trope adds layers of complexity to character relationships, allowing for nuanced exploration of themes such as trust, loyalty, and morality. Characters who experience betrayal are forced to grapple with conflicting emotions and moral dilemmas, leading to compelling internal conflicts and character development arcs. As readers witness how characters respond to betrayal—whether they seek revenge, forgiveness, or redemption—they gain insight into human nature and the complexities of the human psyche, enriching their reading experience and fostering deeper engagement with the story.

What to Watch for When Using the Betrayal Trope

Incorporating the Betrayal trope into a novel can introduce captivating conflicts and complex character dynamics. However, approach this trope with caution to be certain it enhances the narrative rather than falling into clichés or pitfalls that may detract from its impact.

1. **Stereotypical Betrayal Scenarios:** Avoid relying on predictable betrayal clichés, such as the trusted friend turned foe or the romantic partner with hidden ulterior motives. Instead, strive to subvert expectations and craft betrayals that feel authentic and surprising, keeping readers engaged and intrigued.

2. **Lack of Emotional Depth:** Betrayal is a deeply emotional experience, and you must be certain you depict its impact realistically. Be wary of superficial portrayals that fail to explore the profound emotional consequences for both the betrayed and the betrayer. Delve into the characters' motivations, internal conflicts, and moral dilemmas to create a nuanced portrayal of betrayal.

3. **Unrealistic Resolutions:** While betrayal can introduce compelling conflict and tension, be cautious not to resolve betrayals too neatly or conveniently. Avoid rushed reconciliations or overly simplistic resolutions that undermine the complexity of the betrayal. Instead, allow for meaningful exploration of trust, forgiveness, and redemption, acknowledging the aftermath of betrayal may be messy and unresolved.

4. **Overuse of Betrayal as a Plot Device:** Betrayal should serve as a meaningful narrative element rather than a gratuitous plot twist. Be mindful of overusing betrayal to create artificial drama or shock value, as this can diminish its impact and strain credibility. Integrate betrayal organically into the story, ensuring it arises naturally from character motivations and relationships.

When executed skillfully, betrayal can serve as a powerful catalyst for character development, interpersonal conflict, and thematic exploration, enriching the storytelling experience for your readers.

Examples of the Betrayal Trope

Betrayal is a powerful and pervasive theme in mystery fiction, adding depth and complexity to the narrative as characters navigate the treacherous waters of trust and deception. From double-crosses and secret alliances to shocking revelations and hidden motives, betrayal lies at the heart of many compelling mysteries. Here are some examples of the Betrayal trope implemented to captivate readers with tales of intrigue, suspense, and unexpected twists.

- Rachel Watson becomes embroiled in a missing persons investigation after witnessing something suspicious from her train window, in *The Girl on the Train* by Paula Hawkins. The Betrayal trope drives the novel's plot as Rachel uncovers a tangled web of lies and betrayals, leading to a shocking revelation about the true nature of the relationships between the characters.

- In *Big Little Lies* by Liane Moriarty, in a seemingly idyllic Australian suburb, three women become embroiled in a murder investigation that exposes dark secrets and betrayals lurking beneath the surface. The Betrayal trope is used as the novel delves into the complexities of female friendships and the consequences of deception, leading to a shocking climax that upends the lives of the characters involved.

- In Gillian Flynn's *Sharp Objects*, journalist Camille Preaker returns to her hometown to cover the murder of two young girls, uncovering dark secrets and betrayals from her own past in the process. The Betrayal trope is central to the novel as Camille navigates the twisted relationships and hidden agendas of her family and friends, leading to a shocking revelation about the true identity of the killer.

- When a group of elite college students commit a murder, they find themselves bound together by guilt and betrayal, in *The Secret*

History by Donna Tartt. The Betrayal trope is woven throughout the novel as the characters grapple with the consequences of their actions, leading to a tragic and inevitable conclusion that exposes the dark underbelly of privilege and ambition.

Betrayal remains a potent and compelling theme in mystery fiction, driving the plot forward with its twists and turns and keeping readers on tenterhooks until the very end.

Blackmail Trope
(LT, PT, W)

Blackmail Trope Overview

The Blackmail trope is a plot device commonly employed in mystery, thriller, and crime fiction narratives, involving the coercion of individuals through the threat of revealing damaging information or secrets. It introduces tension and moral ambiguity into the storyline, as characters are forced to grapple with ethical dilemmas and confront their past actions. Blackmailers may leverage various forms of leverage, including incriminating photographs, sensitive documents, or personal knowledge, to manipulate their targets into compliance. As the stakes escalate, protagonists must navigate a dangerous web of deceit, betrayal, and hidden agendas to thwart the blackmailer's schemes and protect themselves or others from harm. The resolution of the blackmail mystery often hinges on the uncovering of the blackmailer's identity, motives, and vulnerabilities, leading to a climactic confrontation where secrets are exposed, alliances are tested, and justice is served.

One of the primary sub-genres where the Blackmail trope often features prominently is the traditional whodunit detective mystery. In these stories, the detective protagonist may uncover a web of secrets and deceit, leading to the discovery of blackmail as a motive for the crime at hand. Blackmail serves as a compelling motive, driving characters to desperate measures and creating tension as the detective unravels the truth behind the mystery.

Another sub-genre where the Blackmail trope frequently appears is the legal thriller mystery. In these narratives, blackmail can play a crucial role in courtroom dramas, influencing the decisions and actions of key characters. The revelation of blackmail can turn the tide of a trial, exposing hidden agendas and leading to shocking revelations. The threat of exposure adds layers of suspense and moral ambiguity, challenging characters to confront their own ethical boundaries in the pursuit of justice.

Additionally, the Blackmail trope is often found in psychological thriller mysteries, where it serves as a catalyst for psychological manipulation and power struggles between characters. In these stories, blackmail can be used as a tool for coercion, control, and manipulation, driving characters to confront their darkest secrets and inner demons. The psychological tension created by blackmail adds depth to character dynamics and raises questions about trust, morality, and the nature of evil. Whether used in traditional whodunit detective mysteries, legal thrillers, or psychological thrillers, blackmail adds layers of intrigue, moral ambiguity, and psychological tension to the narrative, keeping readers engaged and guessing until the final reveal.

Why Readers Love the Blackmail Trope

The revelation of blackmail creates a sense of urgency as characters race against time to prevent damaging secrets from being exposed or exploited. This tension keeps readers engaged and invested in the outcome of the story, eager to uncover the truth behind the blackmail scheme.

Additionally, the Blackmail trope often introduces moral ambiguity and ethical dilemmas into the narrative, which have an impact with readers. Characters may be forced to grapple with difficult choices and compromises as they weigh the consequences of their actions. This exploration of moral gray areas adds depth to the characters and raises thought-provoking questions about justice, morality, and the lengths people will go to protect their secrets or achieve their goals.

This trope can be used to explore themes of power dynamics and manipulation within relationships. Characters may find themselves ensnared in a web of manipulation and coercion, forced to confront their vulnerabilities and confrontations. This psychological tension adds complexity to character dynamics and drives the narrative forward as characters navigate the murky waters of deceit and betrayal.

Overall, readers love the Blackmail trope because it enhances the suspense, complexity, and moral ambiguity of mystery novels. By introducing blackmail as a central plot device, authors create a compelling narrative that keeps readers completely engrossed, eager to unravel the secrets and uncover the truth behind the blackmail scheme.

What to Watch for When Using the Blackmail Trope

As with other tropes, there are things you need to be mindful of when incorporating the Blackmail trope into your story. These include:

1. **Clichés and Predictability:** Avoid relying on clichéd scenarios or predictable outcomes when depicting blackmail situations, such as the extramarital affair blackmail scenario that has been done a million times. Instead, strive to inject originality and unexpected twists into the storyline to keep readers engaged and intrigued.

2. **Character Motivations:** Ensure the motivations behind the blackmail are well-developed and plausible. Characters should have clear reasons for resorting to blackmail, and their actions should align with their personalities and backgrounds.

3. **Ethical Considerations:** Explore the ethical implications of blackmail within the narrative. Carefully consider the moral dilemmas faced by characters involved in blackmail, as well as the broader societal and legal consequences of their actions.

4. **Character Agency:** Maintain the agency of characters involved in blackmail situations. Avoid portraying them solely as victims or perpetrators, but rather as complex individuals with agency and autonomy. Allow characters to make meaningful choices and face the consequences of their actions.

5. **Resolution and Consequences:** Provide a satisfying resolution to the blackmail plotline, ensuring loose ends are tied up and unanswered questions are addressed. Consider the long-term consequences of the blackmail scheme on characters and relationships, and depict these repercussions realistically.

The Blackmail trope can add intrigue and suspense to a mystery novel; however, you must approach its execution thoughtfully and with nuance. By avoiding clichés, developing authentic character motivations, addressing ethical considerations, maintaining character agency, and providing a satisfying resolution, you can effectively utilize the Blackmail trope to enhance your storytelling.

Examples of the Blackmail Trope

Blackmail is a potent and suspenseful trope often used in mystery fiction to add layers of intrigue and tension to the narrative. Whether it's a dark secret from the past or compromising information in the present, blackmail drives characters to desperate measures as they navigate the consequences of their actions. Here are some examples:

- In *Strangers on a Train* by Patricia Highsmith, two strangers meet on a train and discuss swapping murders, they unwittingly become entangled in a web of blackmail and betrayal. The Blackmail trope drives the novel's plot as the characters struggle to extricate themselves from the deadly consequences of their fateful encounter, leading to a thrilling and suspenseful climax.

- A group of elite college students commit a murder, only to find themselves bound together by guilt and blackmail, in *The Secret History* by Donna Tartt. The Blackmail trope is woven throughout the novel as the characters grapple with the consequences of their actions, leading to a tragic and inevitable conclusion that exposes the dark underbelly of privilege and ambition.

- In *The Night Manager* by John le Carré, former soldier Jonathan Pine infiltrates the inner circle of a wealthy arms dealer in order to bring him to justice, but soon finds himself caught in a dangerous game of blackmail and betrayal. The Blackmail trope is central to the novel as Pine navigates the murky world of espionage and double-crosses, leading to a thrilling and suspenseful showdown between the forces of good and evil.

Blackmail remains a potent and suspenseful trope in mystery fiction, driving characters to desperate measures as they navigate the consequences of their actions. Whether it's a dark secret from the past or compromising information in the present, the Blackmail trope captivates readers with tales of deception, betrayal, and moral ambiguity.

Cat and Mouse Trope (HCM, PP, PT)

Cat and Mouse Trope Overview

The Cat and Mouse trope is a classic storytelling device that depicts a suspenseful game of wits between two adversaries, often a protagonist and an antagonist. In this dynamic, one character takes on the role of the hunter, while the other becomes the hunted, leading to a tense and exhilarating narrative as they engage in a battle of cunning and strategy. The cat, typically representing the pursuer, employs various tactics to track down and capture the mouse, who in turn uses their ingenuity and resourcefulness to evade capture and outsmart their pursuer. This trope is characterized by a constant shift in power dynamics, as the advantage alternates between the cat and the mouse, keeping audiences rivetted to the story as they anticipate the next move in this high-stakes game. Whether it unfolds in a crime thriller, espionage plot, or psychological drama, the Cat and Mouse trope adds layers of tension and intrigue to the narrative, making it a perennial favorite among audiences seeking suspenseful storytelling.

The Cat and Mouse trope is frequently employed in psychological thrillers, where it serves as a dynamic element in the intricate mind games played between the protagonist and antagonist. In such narratives, the cat represents the cunning and elusive antagonist, while the mouse symbolizes the vulnerable yet resourceful protagonist. As the two engage in a high-stakes battle of wits, readers are drawn into a riveting game of psychological warfare where the stakes are nothing short of life and death.

This trope is also commonly found in police procedurals, particularly in stories involving detectives pursuing cunning criminals. When these criminals are serial killers, we see the Cat and Mouse trope often in serial killer mysteries too. In these narratives, the cat embodies the elusive perpetrator, whose intricate schemes challenge the investigative prowess of the law enforcement team. The mouse, typically represented by the lead detective or protagonist, must navigate a complex web of clues and red herrings to outsmart the adversary and bring them to justice. This trope adds an element of suspense as readers are kept holding their breath, eagerly anticipating the next move in the thrilling game of cat and mouse.

No matter which sub-genre the Cat and Mouse is in, it heightens suspense as the two sides engage in a game of deception and betrayal. Readers are immersed in a world of intrigue, where alliances are fleeting and loyalties are constantly tested. The Cat and Mouse trope heightens the stakes, keeping readers guessing until the final, climactic showdown between the opposing forces.

Why Readers Love the Cat and Mouse Trope

Readers are drawn to the Cat and Mouse trope for its inherent suspense and psychological depth, which creates a gripping narrative experience. One reason for its appeal is the dynamic interplay between the cat and mouse characters, each embodying contrasting traits that drive the conflict forward. The cat represents cunning, unpredictability, and a formidable adversary, while the mouse embodies resilience, intelligence, and the determination to outwit their opponent. This dichotomy creates tension and excitement as readers root for the underdog to outsmart their adversary, leading to a thrilling and unpredictable journey.

The Cat and Mouse trope often features intricate plots and elaborate schemes, keeping readers engaged as they try to unravel the mysteries and anticipate the next move in the game. The constant back-and-forth between the cat and mouse characters, filled with twists, turns, and strategic maneuvers, offers a satisfying intellectual challenge for readers who enjoy deciphering clues and solving puzzles alongside the protagonists. Additionally, the trope allows for exploration of complex themes such as trust, betrayal, and the blurred lines between good and evil, adding depth and nuance to the narrative.

It provides a platform for character development, allowing readers to delve into the psyche of both the protagonist and antagonist as they navigate the intricate dance of deception and pursuit. The psychological tension between the characters, fueled by their conflicting motivations and hidden agendas, adds layers of complexity to the story, making it more compelling and thought-provoking. Ultimately, readers are captivated by the Cat and Mouse trope because it offers a thrilling and immersive experience, combining elements of suspense, intrigue, and psychological depth to create a narrative that keeps them captivated by the narrative until the very end.

What to Watch for When Using the Cat and Mouse Trope

Using the Cat and Mouse trope can be a captivating storytelling technique, but watch for these potential pitfalls:

1. **Character Depth**: While the cat and mouse dynamic drives the plot, it's essential to develop well-rounded characters beyond their roles in the game. Be certain both the cat and mouse have believable motivations, backgrounds, and character arcs to avoid one-dimensional portrayals.

2. **Pacing:** Maintain a balance between tension-building moments and slower, character-driven scenes to keep readers engaged throughout the story. Avoid excessive repetition or predictable patterns in the cat and mouse interactions to prevent the narrative from becoming stagnant.

3. **Resolution:** Provide a satisfying resolution to the cat and mouse conflict that feels earned and logical based on the established character traits and story developments. Avoid rushed or contrived endings that undermine the tension built throughout the narrative.

4. **Moral Complexity:** Explore the moral implications of the cat and mouse game, especially regarding the actions and consequences of both characters. Avoid oversimplifying the dynamics or portraying one side as purely good and the other as purely evil. Instead, embrace the ambiguity and ethical dilemmas inherent in the trope.

Although the Cat and Mouse trope offers thrilling storytelling opportunities, you must navigate it thoughtfully to create a nuanced and compelling narrative. By focusing on character depth, pacing, originality, resolution, and moral complexity, you can harness the tension and excitement of the trope while avoiding common pitfalls.

Examples of the Cat and Mouse Trope

The Cat and Mouse trope is a classic element of mystery fiction, pitting protagonist against antagonist in a thrilling game of wits and strategy. With each move and countermove, tension builds as the stakes are raised and the chase intensifies. Here are some examples of the Cat and Mouse trope:

- In *The Silence of the Lambs* by Thomas Harris, FBI trainee Clarice Starling must outwit incarcerated serial killer Hannibal Lecter in order to catch another murderer known as Buffalo Bill. The Cat and Mouse trope drives the novel's plot as Starling and Lecter engage in a psychological battle of wills, each trying to manipulate the other for their own ends.

- Tom Ripley becomes embroiled in a dangerous game of cat and mouse with law enforcement and his wealthy friend Dickie Greenleaf after assuming Dickie's identity, in *The Talented Mr. Ripley* by Patricia Highsmith. The Cat and Mouse trope is central to the novel as Ripley must stay one step ahead of the authorities while avoiding detection and maintaining his facade.

- In *The Fugitive* by David Baldacci, former CIA agent John Puller becomes the prime suspect and must evade capture while trying to clear his name when his wife is murdered. The Cat and Mouse trope is skillfully employed as Puller engages in a high-stakes game of evasion with law enforcement and pursues leads to uncover the truth behind his wife's death.

The Cat and Mouse trope adds thrills and suspense to narratives, pitting protagonist against antagonist in a high-stakes battle of wits. Whether it's a race against time to catch a killer or a desperate struggle to evade capture, the Cat and Mouse trope keeps readers guessing until the very end.

Cold Case Trope
(AS, HM, PP)

Cold Case Trope Overview

The Cold Case trope refers to unsolved criminal cases, typically homicides or disappearances, that remain open for an extended period, often years or even decades. These cases are considered "cold" because they lack active leads or viable suspects, leading investigators to shelve them indefinitely. Cold cases may involve new evidence, technological advancements, or renewed public interest that prompt law enforcement agencies to reopen investigations and pursue justice for victims and their families. This trope often serves as the backdrop for mystery novels, television shows, and films, where protagonists, such as detectives or amateur sleuths, delve into past events, sift through old evidence, and interview witnesses to uncover long-buried secrets and bring closure to unresolved cases. The Cold Case trope offers storytellers a compelling premise to explore themes of redemption, perseverance, and the enduring quest for truth and justice in the face of seemingly insurmountable obstacles. Additionally, it allows audiences to engage with narratives that blend elements of past and present, offering fresh perspectives on familiar mysteries and challenging preconceived notions about the nature of truth and memory.

The Cold Case trope is typically found in narratives that focus on investigations into unresolved crimes from the past. One sub-genre where this trope frequently appears is the police procedural, where detectives revisit old cases that have remained unsolved for years. These stories delve into the intricacies of forensic analysis, witness interviews, and meticulous detective work as law enforcement officers strive to bring closure to long-forgotten mysteries.

Another sub-genre where the Cold Case trope thrives is the amateur sleuth mystery. In these narratives, amateur detectives or ordinary individuals become embroiled in solving cold cases, often stumbling upon overlooked clues or uncovering new evidence that reopens old wounds. These stories emphasize the protagonist's tenacity and determination to seek justice, even in the face of daunting challenges and personal risks.

The Cold Case trope can also often be found in historical mysteries, where investigators delve into unsolved crimes from bygone eras, exploring the social and cultural contexts of the past to unravel long-buried secrets. These narratives often blend elements of historical fiction with mystery, offering readers a glimpse into the past while unraveling complex puzzles that span generations. Whether set in contemporary times or historical settings, stories featuring the Cold Case trope captivate readers with their blend of suspense, intrigue, and the timeless allure of solving mysteries long thought unsolvable.

Why Readers Love the Cold Case Trope

Narratives using the Cold Case trope stir a sense of intrigue and mystery as they delve into unsolved crimes from the past, presenting readers with puzzles that have remained unresolved for years, if not decades. The allure of uncovering long-buried secrets and piecing together forgotten events adds an element of suspense and excitement to the story, keeping readers engaged as they follow along with the investigation.

It often provides a unique perspective on the criminal justice system, highlighting the complexities of solving crimes that have gone cold over time. Unlike traditional mystery plots that focus on immediate investigations, cold cases require detectives to revisit old evidence, re-interview witnesses, and employ innovative investigative techniques to crack the case. This meticulous approach to solving long-dormant mysteries showcases the dedication and perseverance of law enforcement officers, which readers find both admirable and inspiring.

The Cold Case trope allows for rich character development and exploration of personal motivations. As detectives and amateur sleuths delve into the past, they often confront their own demons and grapple with unresolved issues from their own lives. This introspective journey adds depth to the characters and imbues the narrative with emotional resonance, resonating with readers who appreciate complex, multi-dimensional protagonists.

In the end, the Cold Case trope captivates readers with its blend of historical intrigue, investigative prowess, and emotional depth. By offering a fresh perspective on crime-solving and a window into the past, stories featuring the Cold Case trope provide readers with a satisfying and immersive reading experience that keeps them eagerly turning the pages until the very end.

What to Watch for When Using the Cold Case Trope

When intriguing your readers with the Cold Case trope, there are things you'll need to be on the lookout for, to use this trope effectively. These include:

1. **Maintain Realism:** While fiction allows for creative liberties, maintaining a sense of realism is crucial, particularly when portraying investigative procedures and forensic techniques. Conduct thorough research to be sure accuracy in depicting law enforcement protocols and forensic science.

2. **Balance Past and Present:** A successful Cold Case narrative strikes a balance between exploring the historical events that led to the crime and depicting the present-day investigation. Be careful not to overwhelm readers with excessive flashbacks or backstory, as this can disrupt the pacing of the narrative.

3. **Develop Complex Characters:** In the quest to solve a cold case, characters may grapple with personal demons or unresolved conflicts from their past. However, avoid relying solely on traumatic backstories as a shortcut to character development. Instead, create well-rounded characters with multifaceted motivations and relationships.

4. **Provide Satisfying Closure:** One of the challenges of the Cold Case trope is delivering a satisfying resolution to a long-standing mystery. The conclusion needs to feel earned and plausible, tying up loose ends while still leaving room for ambiguity or emotional resonance.

Take these items into consideration to effectively utilize the Cold Case trope in your novels by exercising creativity, maintaining authenticity, and prioritizing character development and narrative cohesion.

Examples of the Cold Case Trope

The Cold Case trope adds a layer of intrigue and mystery to the narrative, as detectives revisit unsolved crimes from the past, hoping to uncover new evidence and bring closure to long-forgotten cases. From decades-old murders to forgotten disappearances, these stories challenge investigators to unravel the truth and confront the ghosts of the past. Here are a few examples:

- In *The Dry* by Jane Harper, Federal Agent Aaron Falk returns to his drought-stricken hometown to attend the funeral of his childhood friend, who allegedly murdered his family before taking his own life. The Cold Case trope is central to the novel as Falk is drawn into the investigation, uncovering long-buried secrets and questioning the official narrative surrounding the tragic events.

- Detective Rob Ryan returns to his hometown to investigate the murder of a young girl, a case that bears striking similarities to the unsolved disappearance of his childhood friends years earlier, in *In the Woods* by Tana French. The Cold Case trope drives the novel's plot as Ryan grapples with his own traumatic past while delving into the mystery of the present, leading to a shocking revelation that changes everything he thought he knew.

- In *The Crossing Places* by Elly Griffiths, forensic archaeologist Ruth Galloway is called in to assist with the investigation into the discovery of a child's bones near a remote English saltmarsh, a case with eerie parallels to a decades-old disappearance. The Cold Case trope is skillfully employed as Galloway and DCI Harry Nelson uncover clues from the past that shed light on the present, leading to a thrilling and suspenseful conclusion.

The Cold Case trope continues to captivate readers with its tantalizing mysteries and intricate plotlines, challenging detectives to confront the ghosts of the past in their quest for justice. Whether it's a decades-old murder or a long-forgotten disappearance, these six mystery genre books demonstrate the enduring appeal of the Cold Case trope in keeping readers guessing until the very end.

Conspiracies Trope
(HM, NM, OM, PT, STM)

Conspiracies Trope Overview

The Conspiracies trope is a narrative device that revolves around the exploration of secret plots, clandestine organizations, and covert operations within a story's world. It often involves characters uncovering hidden agendas, manipulating events behind the scenes, and navigating webs of deceit and intrigue. Conspiracies can range from political schemes and corporate espionage to paranormal cover-ups and government secrets, adding layers of complexity and mystery to the narrative. This trope thrives on suspense, as characters delve deeper into the shadows to uncover the truth, risking their safety and sanity in pursuit of justice or enlightenment. Whether it's unraveling a centuries-old conspiracy or exposing a contemporary cover-up, stories built around this trope captivate audiences with their suspenseful twists and turns, challenging them to question reality and consider the possibility of hidden forces shaping the world around them.

One common sub-genre where the Conspiracies trope frequently appears is psychological thriller mysteries. In these stories, the conspiracy often revolves around psychological manipulation, gaslighting, or mind games orchestrated by a cunning antagonist. The protagonist may find themselves trapped in a labyrinth of deceit, unsure of who to trust as they unravel the layers of deception and uncover shocking truths about their own psyche. Overall, the Conspiracies trope adds an element of intrigue, suspense, and complexity to mystery stories across various sub-genres. By weaving intricate plots, double-crosses, and hidden agendas, you can keep readers guessing until the final reveal, creating a thrilling and immersive reading experience.

Why Readers Love the Conspiracies Trope

The Conspiracies trope in mystery novels intrigues readers for several compelling reasons. The allure of the unknown and the thrill of uncovering hidden truths captivate readers' imaginations. The idea there may be secret forces at play behind major events or within powerful institutions adds an element of mystery and excitement to the narrative. Readers enjoy the suspense of trying to piece together clues and unravel the intricacies of the conspiracy alongside the protagonist.

This trope often taps into universal themes of distrust in authority and skepticism towards mainstream narratives. In a world where information is easily manipulated and the line between fact and fiction can blur, readers are intrigued by stories that challenge established norms and question the status quo. The idea there may be unseen forces shaping the world around us carries weight with readers who are fascinated by the idea of unearthing hidden truths and exposing corruption.

The Conspiracies trope allows for complex character dynamics and moral ambiguity, which can enrich the storytelling experience. Characters may find themselves torn between loyalty to their beliefs and the consequences of uncovering uncomfortable truths. The moral dilemmas they face, as well as the personal risks they take in pursuit of justice, add depth and nuance to the narrative, keeping readers emotionally invested in the outcome.

It often leads to thrilling plot twists and unexpected revelations, keeping readers turning the page until the very end. The suspense and tension created by the constant threat of betrayal and the unraveling of secrets drive the narrative forward, ensuring readers are engaged and eager to discover the truth. Overall, the Conspiracies trope offers readers an immersive and thought-provoking reading experience that challenges their perceptions and keeps them eagerly turning the pages.

What to Watch for When Using the Conspiracies Trope

When incorporating the Conspiracies trope into your novels, you have the risk of veering into it becoming convoluted if not handled carefully. Be mindful of these potential challenges to maintain reader engagement and credibility.

1. **Avoid Overcomplicating the Plot:** One common pitfall of the Conspiracies trope is the temptation to create overly intricate plots with numerous layers of deception. While complexity can enhance the mystery, it's crucial to strike a balance and ensure the storyline remains coherent and easy for readers to follow. Overcomplicating the plot may lead to confusion and frustration, ultimately detracting from the reader's enjoyment of the story.

2. **Maintain Plausibility:** While conspiracy theories can be inherently far-fetched, you must still strive to maintain a sense of plausibility within your narratives. Readers are more likely to

engage with a story if they find the premise believable and grounded in some semblance of reality. Carefully research your subject matter and avoid relying on outlandish or improbable scenarios that strain credibility.

3. **Develop Well-Rounded Characters:** In the midst of unraveling complex conspiracies, you may inadvertently neglect character development in favor of advancing the plot. However, compelling characters are essential for reader investment and emotional resonance. Be certain your protagonists and supporting cast are well-rounded, with distinct personalities, motivations, and arcs that drive the narrative forward.

4. **Avoid Stereotypical Tropes:** The Conspiracies trope is rife with clichés and stereotypes, from shadowy government agencies to nefarious secret societies. While these elements can be effective when used judiciously, relying too heavily on familiar tropes can lead to predictability and diminish the impact of the story. Strive to bring fresh perspectives and original twists to your conspiracy narratives to keep readers engaged.

With careful planning, attention to detail, and a commitment to authenticity, you can create compelling narratives that captivate readers and leave them eager for more.

Examples of the Conspiracies Trope

Conspiracies are a staple of mystery fiction, weaving intricate webs of deception, intrigue, and hidden agendas that keep readers guessing until the very end. From government cover-ups to secret societies, these stories delve into the shadowy world of conspiracy theories, challenging protagonists to unravel the truth and expose the lies. Here are six examples of mystery genre books that expertly incorporate the Conspiracies trope to captivate readers with tales of suspense and intrigue.

- In *The Da Vinci Code* by Dan Brown, symbolist Robert Langdon is drawn into a deadly race to uncover the truth behind a centuries-old conspiracy involving the Catholic Church and the true identity of Mary Magdalene. The Conspiracies trope drives the novel's plot as Langdon unravels clues hidden in famous works of art and historical landmarks, leading to a shocking revelation that challenges everything he thought he knew.

- Law student Darby Shaw uncovers a conspiracy involving the assassination of two Supreme Court justices, putting her own life in danger as she tries to expose the truth, in *The Pelican Brief* by John Grisham. The Conspiracies trope is central to the novel as Shaw races against time to piece together the puzzle of who is behind the murders and why, leading to a thrilling and suspenseful climax.

- In Jonathan Kellerman's *The Conspiracy Club*, psychologist Jeremy Carrier becomes entangled in a conspiracy involving a series of seemingly unrelated murders, leading him to uncover a secret society with dark and deadly intentions. The Conspiracies trope is central to the novel as Carrier delves into the minds of the killers and their twisted motivations, leading to a thrilling and suspenseful showdown with the forces of evil.

The Conspiracies trope tantalizes readers with its intricate plotlines, challenging protagonists to uncover the truth and expose the lies. Whether it's a centuries-old secret society or a modern-day government cover-up, the Conspiracies trope keeps readers guessing until the very end.

Crime Syndicate Trope
(NM, LT, PP)

Crime Syndicate Trope Overview

The Crime Syndicate trope depicts organized criminal groups or networks that operate with sophisticated tactics and ruthless efficiency, often spanning multiple locations and industries. These syndicates typically engage in a wide range of illicit activities, including drug trafficking, arms smuggling, money laundering, and extortion, among others. Led by powerful and cunning leaders, such as crime bosses or kingpins, these organizations wield significant influence and power, often controlling key aspects of society through bribery, coercion, and corruption. Members of these syndicates are portrayed as cunning and resourceful individuals, skilled in both street smarts and strategic planning, who stop at nothing to achieve their nefarious goals. The presence of a crime syndicate in a narrative adds layers of intrigue and danger, as protagonists must navigate treacherous waters while confronting formidable adversaries who operate outside the bounds of the law.

The Crime Syndicate trope is a common fixture in various mystery sub-genres, often playing a prominent role in stories involving organized crime, corruption, and illicit activities. One sub-genre where this trope frequently appears is the Noir Mystery, known for its gritty, morally ambiguous narratives set against a backdrop of urban decay and criminal underworlds. In these stories, crime syndicates often serve as central antagonistic forces, driving the plot with their nefarious schemes and shadowy operations.

Another sub-genre where the Crime Syndicate trope is prevalent is the Police Procedural, which focuses on the investigative efforts of law enforcement agencies to combat crime. In these narratives, crime syndicates may feature as elusive adversaries, challenging the protagonists with their sophisticated tactics and influence over the criminal underworld. The intricate cat-and-mouse dynamics between law enforcement and organized crime add layers of tension and complexity to the storytelling.

Additionally, the Crime Syndicate trope can be found in the Legal Thriller sub-genre, where legal professionals navigate the intricacies of the justice system to prosecute or defend against criminal charges. In these stories, crime syndicates often serve as targets of legal action, with lawyers and prosecutors striving to dismantle their operations and bring their members to justice. The courtroom battles and legal maneuverings against powerful crime syndicates create compelling narratives of conflict and intrigue.

Why Readers Love the Crime Syndicate Trope

The Crime Syndicate trope captivates readers for several compelling reasons, weaving a web of intrigue, danger, and moral ambiguity that keeps them engrossed in the narrative. At its core, the allure of crime syndicates lies in their portrayal as formidable adversaries, wielding power and influence that rival or even surpass those of the protagonists. This power dynamic sets the stage for high-stakes conflicts and intricate power struggles, creating tension-filled narratives that keep readers eagerly turning the page.

Crime syndicates often embody an aura of mystery and secrecy, shrouding their operations in shadowy intrigue and clandestine dealings. This air of mystique adds an element of unpredictability to the story, as readers are drawn into unraveling the mysteries surrounding the syndicate's motives, methods, and hidden agendas. The enigmatic nature of crime syndicates serves to heighten suspense and anticipation, driving readers to eagerly turn the pages in search of answers.

This trope offers readers a glimpse into the darker aspects of human nature, exploring themes of greed, corruption, and moral ambiguity. By delving into the motivations and inner workings of crime syndicates, you can craft complex characters and morally gray situations that challenge readers' perceptions and provoke thought-provoking discussions about morality and justice. This exploration of ethical dilemmas adds depth and complexity to the narrative, engaging readers on a deeper emotional and intellectual level.

Additionally, readers are drawn to the Crime Syndicate trope for its portrayal of the criminal underworld as a rich and immersive setting ripe with storytelling possibilities. From seedy back alleys to lavish penthouses, crime syndicates inhabit a diverse array of environments that serve as atmospheric backdrops for thrilling and suspenseful tales of intrigue and betrayal. This vivid world-building draws readers into the heart of the action, allowing them to experience the adrenaline-pumping excitement and danger firsthand.

What to Watch for When Using the Crime Syndicates Trope

Introducing crime syndicates into a narrative can infuse a story with intrigue and tension, but you'll need to navigate certain pitfalls to guarantee the trope enhances rather than detracts from your work. Here are some considerations to bear in mind:

1. **Character Depth:** Avoid portraying crime syndicates as one-dimensional entities solely focused on nefarious activities. Be sure members of the syndicate are fleshed-out characters with their own motivations, conflicts, and backstories. Developing well-rounded characters within the syndicate adds depth and complexity to the narrative, elevating it beyond mere stereotypes.

2. **Realism:** While crime syndicates often operate in secrecy and thrive on illicit activities, it's essential to maintain a level of realism in your portrayal. Unrealistic portrayals of crime syndicates can strain the reader's suspension of disbelief and detract from the overall credibility of the story. Conduct thorough research into real-life criminal organizations to create a plausible and authentic depiction.

3. **Balancing Agency:** Be sure protagonists and other characters have agency and autonomy within the narrative, rather than being overshadowed by the power and influence of the crime syndicate. Striking a balance between the formidable nature of the syndicate and the agency of the protagonists allows for compelling conflicts and character development.

4. **Ethical Considerations:** Crime syndicates often engage in illegal and morally dubious activities, presenting you with ethical considerations. Avoid glorifying or romanticizing criminal behavior, and be mindful of the potential impact of depicting violence, drug trafficking, or other illegal activities on readers. Approach sensitive subjects with care and consider the broader ethical implications within the context of the narrative.

Although the Crime Syndicate trope offers rich storytelling opportunities, it's important to navigate potential pitfalls so you can harness the intrigue and tension inherent in crime syndicates to craft compelling narratives that captivate and resonate with readers.

Examples of the Crime Syndicate Trope

Crime syndicates in mystery fiction weave intricate webs of corruption, power, and betrayal that often span multiple novels and series. From organized crime families to secret underground networks, these stories delve into the dark underbelly of society, challenging protagonists to navigate treacherous alliances and dangerous adversaries. Let's look at some examples of how the Crime Syndicate trope to captivate readers with tales of suspense and intrigue.

- In *The Wire in the Blood* by Val McDermid, Detective Chief Inspector Carol Jordan and criminal profiler Tony Hill investigate a series of gruesome murders linked to a dangerous crime syndicate. The Crime Syndicate trope is found as Jordan and Hill delve into the inner workings of the syndicate, uncovering a web of corruption and violence that threatens to consume them both.

- DEA agent Art Keller, in *The Cartel* by Don Winslow, battles the powerful drug cartels of Mexico in this gripping novel that explores the brutal realities of the drug trade. The Crime Syndicate trope is central to the novel as Keller confronts the ruthless leaders of the cartels, navigating a world of corruption, violence, and moral ambiguity in his quest to bring them to justice.

- In *The Black Dahlia* by James Ellroy, Detectives Dwight "Bucky" Bleichert and Lee Blanchard investigate the brutal murder of aspiring actress Elizabeth Short in 1940s Los Angeles, uncovering a tangled web of corruption and deceit that reaches into the highest echelons of society. The Crime Syndicate trope drives the novel's plot as Bleichert and Blanchard navigate the seedy underbelly of Hollywood, confronting corrupt cops, mobsters, and power brokers in their search for the truth.

Crime syndicates remain a compelling and enduring trope in mystery fiction, offering readers a glimpse into the shadowy world of organized crime and the individuals who navigate its dangerous waters. The Crime Syndicate trope often features tales of power, betrayal, and redemption.

Cults and Secret Societies Trope
(GM, OM, PM, PT, STM)

Cults and Secret Societies Trope Overview

The Cults and Secret Societies trope is a fascinating narrative device often woven into stories to add an element of mystery, intrigue, and danger. It revolves around clandestine organizations or groups with hidden agendas, esoteric rituals, and often fanatical followers. These cults and societies operate in the shadows, manipulating events, influencing politics, or pursuing arcane knowledge or power. Characters may find themselves entangled in their web, either as unwitting pawns or as determined investigators seeking to uncover their secrets. The trope awakens feelings of paranoia, suspense, and dread as characters navigate the labyrinthine machinations of these enigmatic groups. Themes of indoctrination, betrayal, and the search for truth often feature prominently, making this trope a rich source of tension and conflict in storytelling.

The Cults and Secret Societies trope is a versatile narrative element that can be found across various mystery sub-genres, adding layers of intrigue, suspense, and conspiracy to the story. One sub-genre where this trope commonly appears is the occult mystery, where secret societies with esoteric beliefs and rituals play a central role in the plot. These clandestine organizations often hold hidden knowledge or arcane powers, driving the protagonist to uncover their mysteries while navigating the dangers of the occult world.

In psychological thrillers, the Cults and Secret Societies trope can manifest as underground groups that manipulate and control individuals for their own nefarious purposes. These organizations may prey on vulnerable characters, exploiting their fears, desires, or vulnerabilities to achieve their sinister objectives. As the protagonist delves deeper into the secrets of these cults, they confront not only external threats but also internal struggles as they grapple with the blurred lines between reality and manipulation.

Another sub-genre where the Cults and Secret Societies trope frequently appears is suspense thriller mysteries, where shadowy cabals and secret societies pull the strings behind the scenes to shape world events. These clandestine organizations operate in the shadows, orchestrating political intrigue, economic manipulation, and even acts of terrorism to further their agendas. As the protagonist uncovers the layers of deception and conspiracy, they must navigate a web of lies and betrayal to uncover the truth and thwart the machinations of those who seek to control the world.

Why Readers Love the Cults and Secret Societies Trope

The Cults and Secret Societies trope has long fascinated readers due to its mysterious and clandestine nature, offering a rich tapestry of intrigue, conspiracy, and suspense. One reason readers are drawn to this trope is the sense of forbidden knowledge and hidden truths it inspires. Cults and secret societies often operate in the shadows, shrouded in secrecy and mystery, leading readers to speculate about what dark secrets they may be harboring. This element of secrecy adds an air of suspense and tension to the narrative, keeping readers engaged as they uncover the truth behind these enigmatic organizations.

This Societies trope taps into our innate curiosity about the unknown and the occult, exploring themes of power, manipulation, and control. Readers are intrigued by the idea of ordinary individuals being drawn into the fold of a cult or secret society, lured by promises of enlightenment or belonging, only to discover the sinister agendas lurking beneath the surface. This exploration of psychological manipulation and the human psyche adds depth to the storyline, allowing readers to delve into the darker aspects of human nature and society.

The Cults and Secret Societies trope also often serves as a vehicle for exploring larger themes such as corruption, betrayal, and the struggle between good and evil. These organizations may be depicted as wielding immense power and influence, posing a threat to the protagonist and society at large. As readers follow the protagonist's journey to uncover the truth and thwart the machinations of these nefarious groups, they are immersed in a thrilling narrative that keeps them on the edge of anticipation. Ultimately, it is the combination of mystery, suspense, and moral ambiguity inherent in the Cults and Secret Societies trope that continues to captivate readers and draw them into its shadowy world.

What to Watch for When Using the Cults and Secret Societies Trope

Exploring the Cults and Secret Societies trope in a novel can be an enticing prospect, offering a wealth of intrigue and suspense for both you and your readers. However, approach this trope with caution to ensure its effective execution and avoid potential pitfalls. Here are some key considerations to keep in mind when incorporating the Cults and Secret Societies trope in your novels:

1. **Depth of Research:** Conduct thorough research into the history, practices, and beliefs of cults and secret societies to guarantee accuracy and authenticity in your portrayal. Misrepresenting these organizations or relying on clichés can undermine the credibility of the narrative and diminish its impact on readers.

2. **Balancing Suspense with Realism:** While suspense is a crucial element of stories involving cults and secret societies, you must strike a balance between maintaining tension and grounding the narrative in realism. Implausible plot twists or overly sensationalized scenarios can strain credibility and detract from the story's impact.

3. **Handling Sensitive Themes:** Cults and secret societies often involve sensitive and potentially triggering themes such as manipulation, abuse, and violence. You must approach these themes with sensitivity and handle them responsibly, avoiding gratuitous depictions or glamorization.

4. **Providing Resolution:** Readers expect a satisfying resolution to the mysteries and conflicts presented in the story. Be certain the protagonist's journey to uncover the truth about the cult or secret society leads to a compelling resolution that ties up loose ends and provides closure for the reader.

While the Cults and Secret Societies trope offers fertile ground for storytelling, approach it with care and attention to detail. With these facets in mind, you'll be able to effectively harness the intrigue of this trope to captivate readers and deliver a compelling narrative.

Cults and secret societies add an element of intrigue and danger to mystery fiction, often serving as the backdrop for tales of hidden agendas, forbidden knowledge, and dark rituals. From ancient brotherhoods to modern-day cults, these stories explore the mysterious and sometimes sinister world of clandestine organizations. Here are some examples of novels that have successfully used this trope:

- In *The Da Vinci Code* by Dan Brown, Robert Langdon teams up with cryptologist Sophie Neveu to unravel the secrets of the Priory of Sion and uncover the truth behind the Holy Grail. The Cults and Secret Societies trope drives the novel's plot as Langdon and Neveu follow a trail of clues left behind by the secretive organization, uncovering hidden messages and symbols that challenge the foundations of Christianity.

- In *The Ninth House* by Leigh Bardugo, Alex Stern, a young woman with the ability to see ghosts, is recruited to monitor the secret societies at Yale University, where dark rituals and occult practices are hidden behind closed doors. The Cults and Secret Societies trope is central to the novel as Stern delves into the sinister world of the societies, uncovering secrets that threaten to consume her and the entire campus.

- Rare book dealer Lucas Corso becomes embroiled in a deadly game of cat and mouse as he investigates a series of murders linked to a mysterious manuscript and a secret society of bibliophiles, in *The Club Dumas* by Arturo Pérez-Reverte. The Cults and Secret Societies trope comes into play as Corso delves into the hidden world of rare books and esoteric knowledge, uncovering secrets that have been buried for centuries.

Cults and secret societies offer a glimpse into the shadowy world of clandestine organizations. The Cults and Secret Societies trope is an excellent way to incorporate suspense, intrigue, and forbidden knowledge.

Kidnapping Trope
(LT, PT, W)

Kidnapping Trope Overview

The Kidnapping trope involves the abduction or unlawful confinement of individuals against their will, serving as a common plot element in various genres, including mystery, thriller, and crime fiction. Whether it's a child taken for ransom, a high-profile kidnapping of a public figure, or a personal vendetta driving the abduction of a loved one, this trope introduces intense drama, suspense, and moral dilemmas into the narrative. Kidnapping plots often feature a race against time as protagonists strive to locate and rescue the victims before it's too late, navigating a treacherous landscape of clues, suspects, and hidden motives. The perpetrators behind the kidnappings may range from opportunistic criminals to shadowy organizations with hidden agendas, adding layers of complexity to the investigation. Ultimately, the resolution of the kidnapping mystery hinges on the ingenuity, resourcefulness, and perseverance of the heroes, as they confront danger, make difficult choices, and uncover the truth behind the abduction.

The Kidnapping trope is a prevalent theme across various mystery sub-genres, often serving as a central plot element that drives the narrative forward. In traditional whodunit detective mysteries, kidnappings frequently occur as the catalyst for the investigation, prompting the protagonist, whether a detective or amateur sleuth, to delve into the mystery surrounding the disappearance of the victim. These stories often involve a race against time as the protagonist works to uncover clues, identify suspects, and rescue the abducted individual before it's too late.

In psychological thrillers, the Kidnapping trope takes on a darker and more nuanced tone, exploring the psychological impact on both the victim and those connected to them. These narratives delve into the complexities of power dynamics, manipulation, and the psychological trauma experienced by both the victim and their loved ones. The focus may shift from the investigation itself to the psychological toll it takes on the characters, offering a deeper exploration of human nature and the lengths to which individuals will go to protect those they care about.

In legal thrillers, the Kidnapping trope often intersects with themes of justice, morality, and the legal system's ability to deliver justice. Kidnappings may be intricately tied to legal cases, serving as a means of coercion, blackmail, or revenge against individuals involved in legal proceedings. These narratives explore the legal and ethical dilemmas faced by lawyers, prosecutors, and judges as they navigate the complexities of the case, often blurring the lines between right and wrong in the pursuit of justice. Once again, this trope serves as a powerful catalyst for suspense, tension, and dramatic conflict, driving the narrative forward while also providing opportunities for exploration of complex themes and character development.

Why Readers Love the Kidnapping Trope

Readers are drawn to the Kidnapping trope for its inherent suspense and tension, which captivate their attention from the outset and keep them eagerly turning the pages. The sudden and unexpected disappearance of a character, particularly one central to the story, creates an immediate sense of urgency and stakes, compelling readers to become emotionally invested in the outcome. This heightened sense of danger and uncertainty drives the narrative forward, keeping readers eagerly reading as they anxiously await the resolution of the kidnapping and the fate of the victim.

It often serves as a catalyst for exploration of complex themes such as power dynamics, morality, and the lengths to which individuals will go to protect their loved ones. Readers are intrigued by the psychological and emotional impact of the abduction on both the victim and those connected to them, offering insight into human nature and the resilience of the human spirit in the face of adversity. The moral dilemmas and ethical questions raised by kidnappings add layers of depth and complexity to the storyline, prompting readers to ponder the nature of justice, revenge, and redemption.

The Kidnapping trope provides ample opportunities for character development and exploration of relationships as characters are forced to confront their deepest fears, vulnerabilities, and secrets in the wake of the abduction. Readers are drawn to the emotional journey undertaken by the characters as they grapple with guilt, grief, and trauma, rooting for their resilience and strength in the face of overwhelming odds. The resolution of the kidnapping often serves as a cathartic moment of triumph and redemption, offering readers a satisfying conclusion to the suspenseful and emotionally charged narrative.

What to Watch for When Using the Kidnapping Trope

When utilizing the Kidnapping trope in your novel, the excitement and tension of this trope must be tempered by the following cautions:

1. **Sensitivity to Real-World Impact:** You must approach the depiction of kidnapping with sensitivity and awareness of its real-world implications. Kidnapping is a traumatic experience with serious emotional and psychological consequences for victims and their loved ones. It's essential to handle the subject matter with care and avoid sensationalizing or glamorizing the ordeal.

2. **Avoiding Gratuitous Violence:** While tension and suspense are integral to the kidnapping trope, refrain from including gratuitous violence or graphic depictions of harm. Instead, focus on the emotional and psychological aspects of the abduction, emphasizing the impact on the characters and their relationships.

3. **Diverse Representation:** When portraying kidnapping victims and perpetrators, strive for diversity and inclusivity. Avoid relying on stereotypes or clichés, and ascertain your characters are depicted with depth and complexity, regardless of their role in the abduction narrative.

4. **Maintaining Plausibility:** The kidnapping plotline should be plausible within the context of the story and the setting. Avoid contrived or unrealistic scenarios that strain credibility, and ensure the motivations and actions of characters remain consistent and believable throughout the narrative.

5. **Respecting Survivor Stories:** If drawing inspiration from real-life kidnapping cases, you must approach the subject matter with respect for the survivors and their experiences. Avoid exploiting or sensationalizing real tragedies for the sake of entertainment, and consider the potential impact of the narrative on survivors and their families.

Although the kidnapping trope can add suspense and drama to a mystery novel, you must approach it with sensitivity, responsibility, and respect for its real-world implications. By keeping these considerations in mind, you can effectively utilize the kidnapping trope while maintaining the integrity and authenticity of your storytelling.

Examples of the Kidnapping Trope

Kidnappings are a compelling and suspenseful plot device often used in mystery fiction to drive tension and propel the narrative forward. From high-stakes ransom scenarios to sinister abductions, these stories explore the harrowing experiences of both the victims and those trying to rescue them. Here are a few examples of mystery genre books that expertly incorporate the Kidnapping trope:

- In *Along Came a Spider* by James Patterson, Detective Alex Cross is drawn into a complex investigation when the daughter of a prominent senator is kidnapped from her exclusive school. The Kidnapping trope comes into play as Cross races against time to track down the kidnapper and unravel the motive behind the abduction, leading to shocking revelations and a thrilling climax.

- In Harlan Coben's *Tell No One*, pediatrician David Beck receives a mysterious email suggesting she may still be alive eight years after her murder. This leads him on a desperate search for answers. The Kidnapping trope is skillfully employed as Beck uncovers shocking secrets and hidden agendas, facing danger at every turn as he races to uncover the truth and rescue his wife from her captors.

- In *The Deep End of the Ocean* by Jacquelyn Mitchard, a family's life is shattered when their three-year-old son disappears during a crowded hotel lobby, leading to a desperate search that spans decades. The Kidnapping trope is used to create an emotional narrative as the family grapples with grief, guilt, and the overwhelming desire to reunite with their lost child, leading to a poignant exploration of love, loss, and resilience.

Whether it's a race against time to rescue the victim or a haunting exploration of the aftermath of captivity, the Kidnapping trope brings to life tales of survival, resilience, and the quest for justice.

MacGuffin Trope
(HCM, HM, W)

MacGuffin Trope Overview

The MacGuffin trope is a narrative device commonly used in mystery, thriller, and adventure stories to drive the plot forward and motivate characters' actions. It refers to an object, goal, or event that serves as the central focus of the story, typically possessing great significance or value to the characters involved, but often ultimately irrelevant to the overall narrative. The term was popularized by filmmaker Alfred Hitchcock, who described it as "the thing that the characters on the screen worry about, but the audience doesn't care." Examples of MacGuffins include coveted treasures, secret documents, or mysterious artifacts your characters pursue or seek to protect throughout the story, often leading to conflict, suspense, and intrigue. While the MacGuffin itself may lack intrinsic importance, its pursuit drives the actions of the characters, creating tension and driving the narrative forward. Ultimately, the resolution of the MacGuffin's significance may vary in importance or impact, with its true value lying in its ability to propel the story and engage the audience in the characters' journey.

The MacGuffin trope is a versatile narrative device that can be found across various mystery sub-genres, adding intrigue and driving the plot forward. In traditional detective whodunit mysteries, the MacGuffin often takes the form of a valuable object or piece of information that serves as the primary focus of the investigation. Detectives may pursue elusive MacGuffins such as stolen jewels, secret documents, or incriminating evidence, leading them on a quest to uncover the truth behind the mystery.

Additionally, the MacGuffin trope can be found in heist and caper mysteries, where it often takes the form of a valuable target that thieves aim to steal or criminals seek to recover. In these stories, the MacGuffin serves as the central objective of the heist, motivating characters to plan elaborate schemes, outwit security measures, and overcome obstacles in pursuit of their goal. The MacGuffin may be a priceless artifact, a cache of stolen money, or a hidden treasure, fueling the tension and suspense as the heist unfolds.

Overall, the MacGuffin trope is a versatile narrative device that transcends specific sub-genres within the mystery genre, enriching stories with suspense, intrigue, and excitement. Whether it's a valuable object, a crucial piece of information, or a coveted target, the MacGuffin drives the plot forward, propelling characters into action and leading readers on an exhilarating journey of discovery and suspense.

Why Readers Love the MacGuffin Trope

Readers are drawn to the MacGuffin trope for its ability to add layers of mystery, suspense, and intrigue to a story. The MacGuffin trope drives the plot forward. It serves as a tangible goal or objective characters pursue throughout the narrative, creating a sense of urgency and propelling the story toward its climax. As readers follow the protagonists' quest to obtain or protect the MacGuffin, they become emotionally invested in the outcome, eagerly turning the pages to see how events unfold.

Another aspect of the MacGuffin trope that appeals to readers is its versatility and potential for creativity. The MacGuffin can take many forms, from ancient artifacts and hidden treasures to classified documents and secret formulas, allowing authors to craft intricate plots filled with twists and turns. This flexibility allows you to tailor the MacGuffin to fit the specific needs of your story, ensuring it serves as a compelling and engaging focal point for the narrative.

This trope often introduces elements of mystery and suspense that keep readers gripped with suspense. As characters race against time to locate the MacGuffin or prevent it from falling into the wrong hands, readers are swept up in a whirlwind of suspenseful twists, unexpected revelations, and thrilling confrontations. The MacGuffin serves as a catalyst for action, driving the story forward and keeping readers guessing until the very end.

Whether it's a valuable artifact, a top-secret formula, or a hidden treasure, the MacGuffin captures the imagination and creates a sense of wonder and excitement that keeps readers coming back for more.

What to Watch for When Using the MacGuffin Trope

Using the MacGuffin trope in a novel can be an effective way to drive the plot forward and captivate readers' attention. However, be wary of the following items to guarantee the trope enhances rather than detracts from the story.

1. **Over-Reliance on the MacGuffin:** While the MacGuffin serves as a central plot device, relying too heavily on it can lead to a

shallow or predictable narrative. Be sure the MacGuffin is integrated organically into the story, and its presence enhances the overall plot rather than overshadowing other elements.

2. **Lack of Originality:** The MacGuffin trope has been used in countless stories across various genres, making it essential for you to put a unique spin on it to avoid clichés and predictability. Try to create a MacGuffin that feels fresh, compelling, and distinct from those seen in other works.

3. **Failure to Provide Satisfactory Resolution:** Readers invest in the MacGuffin's pursuit, expecting a satisfying resolution that justifies the characters' efforts. Be sure the resolution involving the MacGuffin is both logical and emotionally resonant, providing closure and tying up loose ends effectively.

4. **Neglecting Character Development:** In the quest to obtain or protect the MacGuffin, you may inadvertently sideline character development in favor of plot advancement. It's crucial for you to strike a balance between advancing the plot and delving into the characters' motivations, relationships, and growth throughout the story.

5. **Inconsistent Stakes:** The importance of the MacGuffin to the characters and the story's conflict should remain consistent throughout the narrative. Avoid introducing arbitrary changes in the MacGuffin's significance or the characters' motivations, as this can undermine the story's credibility and reader engagement.

While the MacGuffin trope can be a powerful tool for driving the plot and captivating readers, you must navigate its use carefully to avoid common pitfalls. By maintaining originality, balancing plot and character development, and ensuring a satisfying resolution, you can effectively harness the potential of the MacGuffin trope to create compelling and memorable narratives.

Examples of the MacGuffin Trope

The MacGuffin trope motivates characters to pursue their goals. Whether it's a valuable artifact, a hidden treasure, or a coveted piece of information, the MacGuffin propels the narrative forward, leading to twists, turns, and unexpected revelations. Here are some examples of novels that have used the MacGuffin trope effectively:

- *The Maltese Falcon* by Dashiell Hammett, is the quintessential MacGuffin trope mystery novel. Private investigator Sam Spade becomes embroiled in a hunt for a valuable statuette known as the Maltese Falcon, leading to a deadly game of cat and mouse with a cast of shady characters. The MacGuffin trope leads Spade as he navigates a web of deception and betrayal in his quest to uncover the truth behind the elusive falcon.

- In *The Da Vinci Code* by Dan Brown, Robert Langdon races against time to unravel the secrets of the Holy Grail, a mysterious artifact sought after by secret societies and religious extremists. The MacGuffin in this novel is the Holy Grail. It is central to the novel as Langdon and his allies follow a trail of clues left behind by historical figures, uncovering hidden messages and symbols that lead them on a thrilling and suspenseful quest for the truth.

- In a medieval abbey, a series of murders is linked to the discovery of a hidden manuscript rumored to contain dangerous secrets, in

The Name of the Rose by Umberto Eco. The MacGuffin (the manuscript) drives the novel's plot as Franciscan friar William of Baskerville and his novice Adso of Melk unravel the mysteries of the manuscript, leading to a thrilling and suspenseful climax that exposes the truth behind the murders.

The MacGuffin trope remains a potent and captivating element of mystery fiction, driving characters to pursue their goals and unravel the secrets of the plot.

Missing Person Trope
(AS, CM, PP, PT, STM, W)

Missing Person Trope Overview

The Missing Person trope centers around the disappearance of a character, which serves as the central mystery driving the narrative forward. Whether it's a sudden vanishing, a mysterious abduction, or a deliberate disappearance, the absence of the character triggers a chain of events, investigations, and revelations. Often found in mystery novels, thrillers, and crime fiction, this trope introduces tension, suspense, and a sense of urgency as protagonists, detectives, or loved ones race against time to uncover the truth behind the disappearance. The search for the missing person may uncover hidden secrets, long-buried conflicts, and unexpected connections, leading to twists and turns that keep readers engaged. The resolution of the mystery typically provides closure and often reveals the true motivations behind the disappearance, shedding light on the characters' pasts and relationships in the process.

The Missing Persons trope adds layers of intrigue and suspense to the storyline. In traditional detective mysteries, such as police procedurals or amateur sleuth stories, the investigation into a missing person often serves as the central plot, driving the protagonist to unravel the circumstances surrounding the disappearance. The search for answers may lead the detective into a web of secrets and lies, uncovering hidden truths about the missing individual and those connected to them.

In psychological thrillers and suspense mysteries, the Missing Persons trope can take on a more nuanced role, serving as a catalyst for exploring the complexities of human psychology and relationships. The disappearance of a loved one or acquaintance can conjure intense emotions and psychological tension, prompting characters to confront their own fears, guilt, and vulnerabilities. These stories often delve into themes of loss, grief, and the fragile nature of memory, challenging both the characters and readers to question their perceptions of reality.

Additionally, the Missing Persons trope frequently appears in domestic and family-centered mysteries, including classic whodunnits and cozies, where the dynamics of familial relationships are put under the microscope. Family secrets, long-buried resentments, and hidden agendas may come to light as relatives grapple with the sudden absence of a loved one. These narratives often explore the intricacies of family dynamics, portraying the impact of the disappearance on each family member and the ripple effects it has on their lives.

Overall, the Missing Persons trope serves as a versatile narrative tool that can be adapted to fit various mystery sub-genres, offering you a compelling way to explore themes of loss, identity, and the complexities of human nature. Whether driving the plot of a classic whodunit or adding depth to a psychological thriller, the search for a missing person captivates readers with its suspenseful twists and turns, making it a timeless element of mystery fiction.

Why Readers Love the Missing Persons Trope

Readers are drawn to the Missing Persons trope for its ability to kindle a myriad of emotions and generate intense suspense within a story. At its core, the disappearance of a character creates a sense of mystery and intrigue, compelling readers to follow along as protagonists embark on a journey to uncover the truth. The uncertainty surrounding the fate of the missing individual builds tension and anticipation, keeping readers engaged as they eagerly await revelations and plot twists.

This trope often serves as a catalyst for exploring complex themes and issues that connect with readers on a deeper level. For example, stories centered around missing persons can delve into the intricacies of human relationships, portraying the impact of loss and separation on family dynamics, friendships, and communities. Through the lens of a missing person case, you can examine themes of grief, guilt, and resilience, inviting readers to empathize with the characters' struggles and emotional journeys.

The Missing Persons trope offers you a versatile framework for crafting compelling narratives that transcend genre boundaries. Whether featured in traditional detective mysteries, psychological thrillers, or domestic dramas, the search for a missing person provides a compelling backdrop for exploring a wide range of storytelling elements, from intricate plot twists to nuanced character development. This versatility allows you to captivate readers across different genres and demographics, ensuring the appeal of the Missing Persons trope remains enduring and universal.

In the end, readers are drawn to the Missing Persons trope for its ability to captivate their imagination, rouse empathy, and immerse them in intricately woven narratives filled with suspense and emotional depth. As a timeless element of mystery fiction, the search for a missing person continues to strike a chord with audiences, offering an engaging and immersive reading experience that keeps them eagerly turning the pages until the very end.

What to Watch for When Using the Missing Persons Trope

Using the Missing Persons trope can add depth and intrigue to a novel, but following are some challenges to keep in mind when weaving it into your story:

1. **Develop Well-Rounded Characters:** It's essential to create complex and relatable characters involved in the search for the missing person. Ensure their motivations, flaws, and relationships are fleshed out, allowing readers to connect emotionally with their journey.

2. **Maintain Plausibility:** While mystery novels often involve suspending disbelief, it's crucial to maintain a sense of plausibility within the story. Be certain the circumstances surrounding the disappearance and the subsequent investigation are realistic and logically consistent.

3. **Avoid Gratuitous Violence:** Some stories featuring the Missing Persons trope may veer into graphic or sensationalized portrayals of violence. Be mindful of the impact such content may have on readers and strive to handle sensitive themes with care and respect.

4. **Balance Pacing:** The search for a missing person can drive the narrative forward, but pacing is key. Avoid prolonged periods of stagnation or repetitive plot developments by incorporating subplots, twists, and reveals to maintain momentum.

The Missing Persons trope can be a powerful tool for crafting compelling narratives. By infusing your story with depth, originality, and authenticity, you will harness the intrigue of the Missing Persons trope while delivering a satisfying and memorable reading experience for audiences.

Examples of the Missing Persons Trope

The Missing Persons trope is a common and captivating element of mystery fiction, often serving as the catalyst for thrilling investigations and suspenseful narratives. From sudden disappearances to long-standing cold cases, these stories explore the harrowing experiences of those left behind and the relentless efforts to uncover the truth. Here are some examples of the Missing Persons trope:

- In *The Girl on the Train* by Paula Hawkins, Rachel becomes obsessed with the disappearance of a woman named Megan, after witnessing something suspicious from her train window. The Missing Persons trope comes into play as Rachel embarks on her own investigation, uncovering dark secrets and unexpected twists along the way.

- Private investigators Patrick Kenzie and Angela Gennaro are hired to find a missing four-year-old girl named Amanda McCready, in *Gone Baby Gone* by Dennis Lehane. The Missing Persons trope is central to the novel as Kenzie and Gennaro navigate the seedy underbelly of Boston to unravel the truth behind Amanda's disappearance, leading to a morally ambiguous and emotionally charged conclusion.

- In *Sharp Objects* by Gillian Flynn, Journalist Camille Preaker returns to her hometown to cover the disappearance of two young girls, triggering memories of her own troubled past. The Missing Persons trope drives the novel's plot as Preaker delves into the dark secrets of her hometown, uncovering a web of lies and betrayal that threatens to consume her.

The Missing Persons trope drives characters to unravel the truth and confront the dark secrets of the past. Whether it's a sudden disappearance or a long-standing cold case, the Missing Persons trope highlights suspense, intrigue, and the quest for justice.

Political Intrigue Trope
(AS, HM, HBM, PT)

Political Intrigue Trope Overview

The Political Intrigue trope involves the manipulation and maneuvering of power within political circles, where characters engage in complex schemes, alliances, and betrayals to achieve their objectives. This trope often features political leaders, government officials, and other influential figures vying for control, often at the expense of others. Machiavellian tactics, such as deception, blackmail, and sabotage, are commonly employed to gain an advantage or thwart rivals. The narrative may explore themes of corruption, ambition, and morality, as characters navigate the murky waters of politics where loyalty is fleeting, and alliances are forged and broken with little warning. Political intrigue adds layers of tension and suspense to the story, as characters grapple with ethical dilemmas and moral compromises in their quest for power and survival.

The Political Intrigue trope can intertwine with other elements to create rich and multifaceted narratives. It is commonly found in political thrillers, where the intricacies of government, power struggles, and corruption form the backdrop for gripping suspense and high-stakes drama. Within the realm of political mysteries, this trope frequently emerges in stories revolving around political conspiracies, election tampering, or scandals involving public officials. By delving into the murky world of politics, you can explore themes of ambition, betrayal, and moral ambiguity, adding layers of complexity to your narratives.

Additionally, the Political Intrigue trope often intersects with detective fiction, particularly in cases involving crimes with political motivations or implications. Hard-boiled mysteries or amateur sleuths may find themselves embroiled in investigations that lead them into the heart of political machinations, uncovering hidden agendas and exposing the dark underbelly of government institutions. This sub-genre allows you to explore not only the intricacies of solving a mystery but also the broader socio-political landscape in which it unfolds, offering readers a compelling blend of suspense and social commentary.

The Political Intrigue trope can also be prominent in historical mysteries, set against the backdrop of political upheaval, revolutions, or espionage during pivotal moments in history. These stories often feature characters navigating treacherous political landscapes, where loyalties are tested, alliances are forged and broken, and the line between friend and foe becomes increasingly blurred. By immersing readers in meticulously researched historical settings, you can illuminate the complexities of political intrigue while crafting gripping narratives that ring true across time periods. Whether set in the halls of government, the streets of a bustling metropolis, or the corridors of history, stories infused with political intrigue captivate audiences with their potent blend of mystery and social commentary.

Why Readers Love the Political Intrigue Trope

Readers are drawn to the Political Intrigue trope for its gripping portrayal of power struggles, Machiavellian maneuvering, and behind-the-scenes machinations that unfold in the corridors of political power. This trope offers a tantalizing glimpse into the inner workings of governments, institutions, and clandestine organizations, captivating readers with its portrayal of high-stakes conflicts and clandestine agendas. The allure of Political Intrigue lies in its ability to weave intricate webs of deception, betrayal, and manipulation, where every decision carries far-reaching consequences and no one is above suspicion. From political scandals and power grabs to espionage and conspiracy, this trope immerses readers in a world where loyalty is a rare commodity and trust is a luxury few can afford.

This trope often delves into the moral ambiguity of politics, presenting readers with complex characters who navigate ethical dilemmas and moral compromises in their quest for power and influence. Whether it's the idealistic politician torn between principles and pragmatism, the cunning strategist orchestrating a political coup, or the dogged investigator uncovering corruption and scandal, these characters add depth and nuance to the narrative. Readers are fascinated by the psychological dynamics at play, as protagonists grapple with their own ambitions, loyalties, and moral compasses in a world where the line between right and wrong is often blurred.

It provides readers with a front-row seat to the drama, intrigue, and suspense that permeate the political landscape. Through vivid descriptions of political rallies, high-level negotiations, and cloak-and-dagger operations, you transport readers into a world where power is wielded like a weapon and secrets lurk behind every closed door. This sense of intrigue and suspense keeps readers eagerly turning pages, as they become embroiled in the twists and turns of political maneuvering and the quest for power. The Political Intrigue trope connects with readers due to its portrayal of power dynamics, moral complexity, and high-stakes conflicts that unfold in the world of politics. By offering a glimpse into the clandestine world of political intrigue, this trope provides readers with a compelling exploration of ambition, betrayal, and the pursuit of power, making it a perennial favorite among fans of mystery and suspense fiction.

What to Watch for When Using the Political Intrigue Trope

When incorporating the Political Intrigue trope into your novels, there are facets that can affect the effectiveness and authenticity of your storytelling. Here are some key considerations to keep in mind:

1. **Complex Plotting:** One common challenge you face with Political Intrigue is maintaining a coherent and engaging plot amidst the intricacies of political maneuvering. Avoid convoluted storylines that confuse readers and detract from the central narrative. Strive for clarity and coherence in plotting, ensuring each twist and turn serves to advance the story rather than bog it down with unnecessary complexity.

2. **Character Development:** In the world of Political Intrigue, characters often hold multiple allegiances, motivations, and hidden agendas. You must carefully develop your characters to guarantee they remain compelling and relatable amidst the political machinations. Avoid caricatures or stereotypes, and instead focus on creating multidimensional characters with believable motivations and inner conflicts.

3. **Realism vs. Dramatic License:** While Political Intrigue offers ample opportunities for drama and suspense, strike a balance

between realism and dramatic license. Avoid exaggerating or sensationalizing political events for the sake of plot convenience, as this can undermine the credibility of the narrative. Instead, strive for authenticity by grounding the story in real-world political dynamics and historical context.

4. **Research and Accuracy:** Political settings can be complex and nuanced, requiring thorough research to accurately portray the intricacies of government, diplomacy, and power dynamics. Invest time in researching political systems, protocols, and procedures to guarantee your portrayal is credible and plausible. Avoid factual inaccuracies or misrepresentations that may detract from the reader's immersion in the story.

5. **Handling Sensitive Topics:** Political themes often touch upon sensitive or controversial issues, such as corruption, conspiracy, and abuse of power. Approach these topics with sensitivity and nuance, avoiding gratuitous depictions of violence or exploitation. Exercise caution when depicting real-world political events or figures, ensuring your portrayals are respectful and balanced.

By avoiding common pitfalls such as convoluted plotting, shallow characterizations, and factual inaccuracies, you will be able to create compelling narratives that captivate readers with your authenticity and depth.

Examples of the Political Intrigue Trope

Political intrigue is a riveting and captivating element often found in mystery fiction, weaving tales of power, deception, and betrayal within the corridors of government and beyond. From political scandals to clandestine operations, these stories delve into the murky world of politics, where nothing is as it seems and trust is a rare commodity. Following are some examples:

- In *The Pelican Brief* by John Grisham, law student Darby Shaw uncovers a conspiracy involving the assassination of two Supreme Court justices, leading to a dangerous game of cat and mouse with powerful forces. The Political Intrigue trope drives the novel's plot as Shaw races against time to expose the truth, navigating a web of corruption and betrayal that reaches the highest levels of government.

- A professional assassin known as the Jackal is hired to kill French President Charles de Gaulle, setting off a tense and suspenseful race to thwart the plot, in *The Day of the Jackal* by Frederick Forsyth. The Political Intrigue trope is central to the novel as the Jackal navigates a world of political maneuvering and espionage, using deception and cunning to evade capture and carry out his deadly mission.

- In *Absolute Power* by David Baldacci, master thief Luther Whitney witnesses the murder of a woman by the President of the United States, setting off a chain of events that exposes corruption and cover-ups within the highest echelons of power. The Political Intrigue trope is used as Whitney becomes embroiled in a dangerous game of cat and mouse with powerful government officials, risking his life to uncover the truth and seek justice.

Political intrigue remains a captivating and suspenseful trope in mystery fiction, offering readers a glimpse into the murky world of power, deception, and betrayal.

Race Against Time Trope (HCM, LT, PP, PT, SKM, STM)

Race Against Time Trope Overview

The Race Against Time trope is a storytelling device commonly used in various genres, including mystery, thriller, action, and adventure. It revolves around characters striving to accomplish a critical task or achieve a specific goal within a limited timeframe, typically facing imminent danger or dire consequences if they fail to succeed in time. This trope creates tension, urgency, and suspense as protagonists must overcome obstacles, navigate challenges, and make difficult decisions while under pressure. The narrative often unfolds in a fast-paced manner, with the clock ticking down relentlessly, heightening the stakes and driving the sense of urgency for both the characters and the audience. Whether it's defusing a bomb, thwarting a villain's sinister plot, or rescuing a kidnapped loved one, the Race Against Time trope keeps readers hanging on every word, eagerly anticipating the outcome of the high-stakes race against the clock.

The Race Against Time trope is found in mystery sub-genres where urgency and suspense are paramount. One common sub-genre where this trope frequently appears is the thriller subsets of mystery, like the psychological thriller and legal thriller sub-genres. In these stories, protagonists often find themselves in a high-stakes situation where they must solve a mystery or prevent a crime before it's too late. The tension is heightened as the clock ticks down, and the protagonist races against time to uncover clues, outsmart adversaries, and avert disaster.

Another sub-genre where the Race Against Time trope is prevalent is the suspense thriller mystery. These stories typically involve a protagonist who becomes entangled in a dangerous situation with a looming deadline. Whether it's a bomb threat, a kidnapping, or a deadly virus outbreak, the protagonist must act swiftly and decisively to save themselves and others. The constant pressure of time adds an extra layer of intensity to the narrative, keeping readers completely absorbed until the very end.

The Race Against Time trope often also features prominently in police procedural mysteries. In these stories, law enforcement officials are tasked with solving a crime within a limited timeframe, such as before a statute of limitations expires or before a killer strikes again. Detectives must navigate through red herrings and dead ends while facing mounting pressure from their superiors and the public. The race to catch the culprit before it's too late drives the narrative forward and creates a sense of urgency that propels the story toward its climax.

In conclusion, the Race Against Time trope is a versatile device that can be found across various mystery sub-genres, including Thriller, Suspense, and Police Procedural mysteries. Whether it's a lone detective chasing a serial killer or a group of protagonists racing to prevent a catastrophe, this trope injects tension and excitement into the narrative, keeping readers hooked from beginning to end.

Why Readers Love the Race Against Time Trope

The Race Against Time trope creates a sense of urgency and suspense that keeps readers engaged throughout the story. This trope introduces a ticking clock element, where characters must act quickly to achieve their goals or prevent a disaster from occurring. The looming deadline adds an extra layer of tension, making every moment feel crucial and heightening the stakes for the protagonists. As readers follow the characters' frantic efforts to beat the clock, they experience a thrilling adrenaline rush that keeps them eagerly turning the pages.

It often forces characters to confront their limitations and push themselves beyond their comfort zones. Whether it's a detective racing to solve a case before a killer strikes again or a protagonist trying to defuse a bomb before it detonates, the pressure of time compels characters to make split-second decisions and take bold risks. This aspect of the trope can lead to compelling character development as readers witness the protagonists' resilience, resourcefulness, and determination in the face of adversity.

Furthermore, the Race Against Time trope taps into universal fears and anxieties about mortality and the fragility of life. The idea of running out of time hits home with readers on a visceral level, prompting them to empathize with the characters' desperate struggle to defy fate and seize control of their destiny. This emotional connection deepens the reader's investment in the story and intensifies their desire to see the protagonists succeed against all odds. Ultimately, it is this combination of gripping tension, character-driven drama, and existential themes that makes the Race Against Time trope a perennial favorite among mystery readers.

What to Watch for When Using the Race Against Time Trope

When utilizing the Race Against Time trope in your novel, keep these key considerations in mind:

1. **Unrealistic Timelines:** Ensure the time constraints imposed on the characters are plausible within the context of the story. If the deadline feels arbitrary or too conveniently aligned with the plot, it can strain believability and undermine the tension of the race against time.

2. **Lack of Character Development:** While the urgency of the situation may drive the plot forward, don't neglect opportunities for character development. It's essential to balance the action-packed sequences with moments of introspection and emotional depth to be sure your readers remain invested in the characters' journey.

3. **Predictability:** The Race Against Time trope is a familiar narrative device, and readers may anticipate certain plot twists or outcomes. Try to incorporate unexpected obstacles and complications to keep the story fresh and unpredictable, avoiding clichés and formulaic resolutions.

4. **Overreliance on Tension:** While tension is a central element of the trope, an excessive focus on urgency and suspense can become exhausting for readers if not tempered with moments of relief and resolution. It's crucial to vary the pacing and tone of the narrative to maintain engagement without overwhelming the audience.

5. **Ignoring Consequences:** The consequences of failing to meet the deadline should be clearly established and carry weight throughout the story. Avoid resorting to convenient solutions or last-minute rescues that undercut the impact of the characters' actions and decisions.

Although the Race Against Time trope can add excitement and urgency to a novel, approach it with care to be sure its effectiveness in driving the narrative forward. By maintaining a balance between tension, character development, and plot twists, you can harness the full potential of this trope to captivate readers and deliver a compelling storytelling experience.

Examples of the Race Against Time Trope

The Race Against Time trope is a thrilling and adrenaline-fueled element commonly found in mystery fiction, where protagonists must solve a mystery or prevent a disaster before it's too late. From ticking time bombs to imminent threats, these stories keep readers totally captivated as characters race against the clock to uncover clues, thwart villains, and save the day. Following are some examples of novels using this trope to fill their tales with suspense and urgency.

- In *Angels & Demons* by Dan Brown, Harvard symbologist Robert Langdon races against time to stop a secret society from carrying out a deadly plot to destroy the Vatican. The Race Against Time trope is the central plot device as Langdon deciphers ancient clues and navigates the labyrinthine streets of Rome, facing danger at every turn as he races to prevent a catastrophic event.

- In Dean Koontz's *Ticktock*, a writer and a photographer find themselves in a deadly game of cat and mouse with a deranged killer who leaves a ticking clock at each crime scene. The Race Against Time trope drives the novel's plot as the protagonists race to uncover the identity of the killer and stop him before he claims his next victim, leading to a suspenseful and pulse-pounding showdown.

- A team of scientists must race against time to contain a deadly extraterrestrial microorganism before it wipes out all life on Earth, in *The Andromeda Strain* by Michael Crichton. The Race Against Time trope is featured as the scientists work frantically to analyze the organism and develop a cure, facing numerous obstacles and setbacks along the way in their desperate bid to save humanity.

Whether it's stopping a deadly plot or uncovering the truth before it's too late, the Race Against Time trope creates tales of urgency, danger, and heroism.

Red Herring Trope
(AS, CM, HM, PM, PP, PT, W)

The Red Herring trope is a narrative device used in storytelling, particularly in mystery and thriller genres, to mislead the audience or characters by introducing false clues or distractions that divert attention away from the true solution to the mystery. The term "red herring" originates from the practice of using a strong-smelling cured fish to divert hunting dogs from the scent of their prey. In literature, red herrings are often employed to create suspense and challenge the audience's ability to discern the truth from deception. These false leads are typically presented as plausible explanations or suspects but are ultimately revealed to be irrelevant or misleading. Red herrings serve to heighten tension, prolong suspense, and keep readers or viewers engaged in the mystery by adding layers of complexity to the plot. Effective use of red herrings requires careful balancing to maintain believability while keeping the true solution hidden until the climax of the story.

The Red Herring trope, known for its misleading clues or characters designed to divert attention from the true culprit, is a staple in various mystery sub-genres. In classic whodunit mysteries, such as traditional detective stories or cozy mysteries, red herrings are frequently employed to keep readers guessing until the final reveal. These misdirections add layers of complexity to the plot and heighten suspense as the protagonist sifts through false leads to uncover the truth. In psychological thrillers, where the focus often lies on the protagonist's state of mind, red herrings serve to blur the line between reality and illusion, leaving both the character and the reader uncertain about what to believe.

In police procedurals, the Red Herring trope plays a crucial role in the investigation process, as law enforcement officers must navigate through multiple suspects and motives to identify the real perpetrator. The inclusion of false clues and suspicious characters adds depth to the procedural narrative, showcasing the challenges and complexities of solving crimes within a bureaucratic framework. Moreover, in legal thrillers, red herrings are frequently used to create doubt and uncertainty in the courtroom, as attorneys manipulate evidence and testimony to sway the jury in their favor.

In paranormal mysteries, the Red Herring trope takes on a unique dimension, often blurring the lines between the natural and the supernatural. As protagonists grapple with otherworldly phenomena and unexplained occurrences, false leads and misleading clues add an additional layer of mystery to the narrative, keeping readers engaged and intrigued by the unknown. Overall, the Red Herring trope serves as a versatile tool for mystery writers across various sub-genres, allowing them to craft intricate plots and keep readers rivetted to the story until the very end.

Why Readers Love the Red Herring Trope

The Red Herring trope is a reader favorite for a variety of reasons. It adds an element of excitement and challenge to the story. By introducing false leads and misleading clues, the narrative becomes more intricate, prompting readers to engage actively in solving the mystery alongside the protagonist. This interactive aspect of storytelling can be highly rewarding for readers, as they relish the opportunity to test their deductive skills and unravel the truth hidden amidst the deception.

Additionally, the Red Herring trope heightens suspense and tension within the narrative. As readers encounter various suspects and potential motives, they are kept on edge, eagerly anticipating the moment when the true culprit will be revealed. This anticipation builds throughout the story, creating a sense of anticipation and excitement that compels readers to keep turning the pages. The uncertainty surrounding the identity of the perpetrator adds an air of unpredictability to the plot, ensuring readers remain engaged until the very end.

This trope adds depth to the characters and the overall story arc. As protagonists navigate through false leads and conflicting evidence, their development as sleuths is often put to the test. They must demonstrate critical thinking, resilience, and perseverance in the face of adversity, qualities readers admire and root for. Additionally, the presence of red herrings can lead to unexpected plot twists and revelations, keeping the story dynamic and unpredictable.

Overall, readers love the Red Herring trope because it enhances the mystery-solving experience, heightens suspense, and adds complexity to the narrative. By challenging readers to distinguish between truth and deception, this trope invites them on a thrilling journey of discovery, where every clue and revelation brings them one step closer to unraveling the mystery.

On the surface, the Red Herring trope appears to be one of the simpler tropes to incorporate in your writing. Add some misleading clues and there you have it, right? Wrong. To effectively implement the Red Herring in your novels, be certain to consider these items:

1. **Overuse:** While red herrings can add intrigue to a narrative, using them excessively can overwhelm readers and dilute the impact of genuine plot twists. Strike a balance between misleading clues and genuine evidence to maintain suspense without leading readers astray.

2. **Lack of Clarity:** Red herrings should serve to challenge readers' assumptions and keep them guessing, but you must guarantee the narrative remains coherent. Confusing or ambiguous clues may frustrate readers and detract from their enjoyment of the story.

3. **Unconvincing Motives:** The motivations behind red herrings should be plausible within the context of the story. If characters act in ways that seem contrived or inconsistent with their established personalities, readers may find it difficult to suspend their disbelief.

4. **Neglecting Resolution:** While red herrings can create tension and uncertainty, it's essential to tie up loose ends and provide a satisfying resolution. Leaving too many unanswered questions or unresolved plot points can leave readers feeling unsatisfied and may undermine the impact of the story's climax.

5. **Predictability:** A well-executed red herring should surprise and challenge readers, but if it's too predictable, its effectiveness may be diminished. Strive to introduce red herrings that are unexpected yet plausible, keeping readers engaged and invested in the mystery.

While the Red Herring trope can add depth and intrigue to a mystery novel, you must use it judiciously and with careful consideration of its impact on the narrative. By avoiding common pitfalls such as overuse, lack of clarity, and unconvincing motives, you can harness the power of red herrings to captivate readers and enhance the overall reading experience.

Examples of the Red Herring Trope

The Red Herring trope is used by authors to introduce false clues or suspects to mislead readers and keep them guessing until the very end. These deceptive elements add layers of complexity to the plot, leading readers down unexpected paths and heightening the suspense of the narrative. Here are a few examples of mysteries with the Red Herring trope woven into the narrative:

- In *Gone Girl* by Gillian Flynn, Nick Dunne becomes the prime suspect in the disappearance of his wife, Amy, but as the investigation unfolds, it becomes clear not everything is as it seems. The Red Herring trope is seen as Flynn introduces multiple twists and false leads, keeping readers guessing about the true nature of Amy's disappearance until the shocking conclusion.

- In the classic mystery *The Hound of the Baskervilles* by Arthur Conan Doyle, Sherlock Holmes investigates the mysterious death of Sir Charles Baskerville, which is believed to be the work of a supernatural hound haunting the family estate. Holmes navigates a web of deceit and intrigue, uncovering false leads and red herrings planted by the true culprit to divert suspicion.

- Agatha Christie's *The Murder of Roger Ackroyd* finds renowned detective Hercule Poirot investigating the murder of wealthy industrialist Roger Ackroyd. He uncovers a web of secrets and lies within his family and household staff that leads readers on a twisted journey of deception and betrayal until the shocking revelation of the true killer.

The Red Herring trope adds depth and intrigue to the narrative as authors skillfully weave false clues and deceptive characters into the plot. Whether it's a murder investigation or a complex puzzle to solve the Red Herring trope adds suspense, deception, and unexpected twists.

Revenge Trope
(HBM, LT, PP, PT, STM)

Revenge Trope Overview

The Revenge trope is a compelling narrative element frequently employed in storytelling across various genres, from thrillers and dramas to fantasies and mysteries. It centers on a character's relentless pursuit of vengeance against those who wronged them, often driven by deep-seated anger, trauma, or a thirst for justice. Revenge plots typically involve intricate schemes, calculated maneuvers, and moral dilemmas as characters grapple with the consequences of their actions. This trope can serve as a powerful motivator for characters, propelling them on a journey of self-discovery, redemption, or descent into darkness. The pursuit of revenge often leads to intense confrontations, moral ambiguity, and unexpected twists, keeping audiences engaged and invested in the outcome. Ultimately, the resolution of the revenge trope raises thought-provoking questions about morality, justice, and the human condition, offering insights into the complexities of human nature.

In traditional detective fiction, such as hard-boiled mysteries or police procedurals, the Revenge trope often manifests as a motive driving both perpetrators and victims. Whether seeking vengeance for past wrongs or perceived injustices, characters driven by revenge can add layers of complexity to investigations, blurring the lines between perpetrator and victim.

Within psychological thrillers and suspense thriller mysteries, the Revenge trope takes on a more personal and intimate tone, often revolving around individuals seeking retribution for personal betrayals or traumas. These narratives delve deep into the psyche of both avengers and their targets, exploring themes of morality, justice, and the consequences of unchecked vendettas. As the pursuit of revenge escalates, tensions rise, and characters are forced to confront their darkest desires and motivations.

In the realm of legal thrillers, the Revenge trope frequently underpins intricate plots involving legal battles, corporate espionage, or high-stakes conflicts. Whether seeking to settle scores in the courtroom or through extralegal means, characters driven by revenge navigate complex legal landscapes where justice and morality are often elusive. These narratives often highlight the ethical dilemmas inherent in seeking revenge within the confines of the law, as well as the blurred boundaries between justice and vengeance.

Why Readers Love the Revenge Trope

The allure of the Revenge trope lies in its potent cocktail of emotion, drama, and catharsis, captivating readers with its primal appeal and visceral impact. At its core, the desire for revenge taps into universal human experiences of betrayal, injustice, and wounded pride, resonating deeply with readers on an emotional level. The journey of a character seeking retribution often ellicits empathy and sympathy from readers, who vicariously experience the highs and lows of their quest for justice.

The Revenge trope offers a compelling exploration of complex moral and ethical dilemmas, forcing readers to grapple with questions of right and wrong, justice and vengeance. As characters navigate the murky waters of revenge, readers are drawn into a morally ambiguous world where the lines between hero and villain blur, challenging their preconceived notions of morality and justice. This moral ambiguity adds layers of depth and nuance to the narrative, keeping readers engaged as they ponder the ethical implications of the characters' actions.

Additionally, it provides a satisfying narrative arc characterized by tension, suspense, and ultimately, resolution. As readers follow the protagonist's journey from victim to avenger, they become invested in the outcome, eagerly anticipating the moment when justice will be served or vengeance exacted. The cathartic release of seeing the antagonist get their comeuppance or the protagonist achieve closure can be immensely satisfying for readers, offering a sense of closure and emotional fulfillment that leaves a lasting impression.

Ultimately, readers love the Revenge trope for its ability to tap into primal human emotions, explore complex moral quandaries, and provide a cathartic journey of justice and redemption. Whether unfolding in the gritty streets of a hard-boiled mystery or the hallowed halls of a legal thriller, stories driven by the desire for revenge resonate with readers by offering a potent blend of emotion, drama, and moral complexity that keeps them eagerly turning the pages until the very end.

What to Watch for When Using the Revenge Trope

Navigate the Revenge trope with care to ensure its integration into the narrative feels organic and thematically resonant. By exploring the multifaceted motivations behind acts of revenge and the far-reaching consequences for both individuals and society, you can harness the power of this trope to craft compelling stories that connects with readers long after the final page is turned. Here are a few items to be wary of:

1. **Over-Reliance on Vengeance:** While revenge can be a powerful motivator for characters, relying too heavily on this trope can lead to predictable plotlines and one-dimensional characters. Be sure the desire for revenge is just one aspect of your characters' motivations and not the sole driving force behind their actions.

2. **Lack of Character Development:** Characters seeking revenge should undergo meaningful growth and transformation throughout the story. Avoid portraying them as static avengers consumed by their quest for retribution. Instead, characters should grapple with moral dilemmas, confront their own flaws and vulnerabilities, and ultimately evolve in response to their experiences.

3. **Unrealistic Portrayals of Revenge:** Revenge stories often walk a fine line between satisfying catharsis and gratuitous violence. Be mindful of depicting revenge in a way that feels authentic and justified within the context of the narrative. Gratuitous violence or excessive retribution can alienate readers and undermine the emotional impact of the story.

4. **Oversimplification of Moral Ambiguity:** The pursuit of revenge inherently raises complex moral questions, but resist the temptation to oversimplify these dilemmas. Characters grappling with revenge should confront nuanced ethical considerations, and the narrative should allow for shades of gray rather than presenting a black-and-white view of morality.

5. **Neglecting Consequences:** Revenge is rarely a straightforward path; explore the consequences of characters' actions in a realistic manner. Whether it's legal repercussions, emotional fallout, or unintended collateral damage, the consequences of seeking revenge should be integral to the story and contribute to its depth and complexity.

While the Revenge trope can add depth and intensity to a narrative, approach it with care to avoid common pitfalls. By developing multifaceted characters, exploring complex moral dilemmas, and realistically portraying the consequences of revenge, you can harness the power of this trope to create compelling and thought-provoking stories that strike a chord with readers long after the final page.

Examples of the Revenge Trope

Revenge is a powerful and compelling theme often explored in mystery novels, driving characters to seek retribution for past wrongs and injustices. From long-standing vendettas to personal vendettas, these stories delve into the darker aspects of human nature, where the desire for vengeance consumes protagonists and fuels their actions. Here are a few examples:

- In *The Count of Monte Cristo* by Alexandre Dumas, after being wrongfully imprisoned for years, Edmond Dantès escapes and seeks revenge against those who betrayed him. The Revenge trope is used as Dantès meticulously plans and executes his vengeance, leading to a thrilling and morally ambiguous journey of justice and redemption.

- After being inexplicably imprisoned for fifteen years, Oh Dae-su seeks revenge against his captors and uncovers the shocking truth behind his incarceration, in *Oldboy* by Garon Tsuchiya and Nobuaki Minegishi. Dae-su embarks on a violent and harrowing journey of redemption, confronting his past and seeking justice for the injustices he has suffered.

- In *The Reversal* by Michael Connelly, prosecutor Mickey Haller seeks revenge against a defense attorney who previously manipulated him in court, leading to a tense and morally complex legal showdown. Haller navigates the intricacies of the legal system and grapples with his own ethical dilemmas, leading to a gripping and suspenseful climax.

Revenge is a timeless and captivating theme in mystery novels, driving characters to confront their past and seek justice for past wrongs. The Revenge trope adds suspense, moral complexity, and the human desire for retribution to any storyline.

Stolen Identity Trope
(LT, PT)

Stolen Identity Trope Overview

The Stolen Identity trope is a narrative device frequently employed in mystery and thriller genres to explore themes of deception, betrayal, and personal identity. In this trope, a character's identity is unlawfully appropriated by another individual, leading to a series of complex and often perilous consequences. Whether it's through identity theft, forgery, or manipulation of personal information, the victim finds themselves ensnared in a web of deceit as their name, reputation, and even their very existence are called into question. The stolen identity may be used for various nefarious purposes, such as committing crimes, evading capture, or assuming a new persona altogether. As the victim struggles to reclaim their true identity and untangle themselves from the web of lies, they are forced to confront their own vulnerabilities and grapple with the repercussions of having their identity stolen. This trope often serves as a catalyst for thrilling plot twists, unexpected revelations, and intense psychological drama as characters navigate the murky waters of deception and betrayal.

The Stolen Identity trope finds its home in various mystery sub-genres, each offering unique contexts and opportunities for exploration. One of the most common sub-genres where this trope is prevalent is psychological thriller mysteries. In these stories, the stolen identity serves as a catalyst for intense psychological drama, blurring the lines between reality and illusion. Characters grapple with their own sense of self and struggle to discern friend from foe, adding layers of complexity to the plot.

The legal thriller genre also provides fertile ground for the exploration of the Stolen Identity trope. In these stories, the stolen identity may be used to frame an innocent person for a crime they did not commit or to conceal the true identity of a perpetrator. Lawyers and investigators must unravel the web of deception to uncover the truth and secure justice for their clients. The legal thriller genre often delves into themes of corruption, power, and the flaws of the justice system, offering readers a thought-provoking exploration of morality and ethics. The Stolen Identity trope's ability to generate suspense, explore complex psychological dynamics, and raise thought-provoking questions about identity and trust makes it a compelling element in mystery storytelling.

Why Readers Love the Stolen Identity Trope

Readers are drawn to the Stolen Identity trope for its inherent sense of mystery, intrigue, and suspense, which captivate their imagination and keep them eagerly turning pages. At its core, this trope revolves around the notion of someone assuming the identity of another person, leading to a myriad of possibilities for deception, betrayal, and unexpected twists. The idea of living a double life, where the lines between truth and falsehood blur, adds layers of complexity to the narrative, making it inherently compelling.

One reason readers love the Stolen Identity trope is the element of psychological tension it brings to the story. As characters grapple with questions of identity, trust, and betrayal, readers are drawn into a web of uncertainty, questioning the authenticity of every interaction and revelation. This psychological depth adds depth to the characters and their relationships, creating a rich tapestry of emotions that hits home with readers on a visceral level.

It also often serves as a vehicle for exploring themes of identity, self-discovery, and the nature of truth. As characters navigate the fallout of a stolen identity, they are forced to confront their own vulnerabilities, insecurities, and moral dilemmas, leading to moments of profound introspection and personal growth. Readers are drawn to these thematic explorations, as they provide insights into the human condition and challenge their own perceptions of identity and reality.

Another aspect that appeals to readers is the element of suspense and unpredictability inherent in the Stolen Identity trope. As the plot unfolds, readers are kept with their hearts pounding, eagerly anticipating the next twist or revelation that will shed light on the true identity of the characters involved. This sense of anticipation and uncertainty drives the narrative forward, keeping readers engaged and invested in unraveling the mystery at the heart of the story. By delving into the complexities of human nature and the blurred lines between truth and deception, this trope offers readers a compelling journey filled with twists, turns, and unexpected revelations that leave a lasting impression long after the final page is turned.

What to Watch for When Using the Stolen Identity Trope

When incorporating the Stolen Identity trope into your novels, it's important to be certain the narrative remains engaging and credible. While this trope can add layers of intrigue and suspense to a story, it also carries the risk of veering into cliché or implausibility if not handled carefully. Here are key considerations for writers looking to utilize the Stolen Identity trope effectively:

1. **Maintain Consistency and Believability:** The Stolen Identity trope relies on a suspension of disbelief from readers, but this suspension can quickly unravel if the narrative lacks consistency or fails to adhere to basic principles of plausibility. Carefully establish the rules of their fictional world and be certain the actions and behaviors of characters remain consistent within that framework. Any deviations from established norms should be logically justified to maintain reader engagement.

2. **Handle Sensitive Themes with Care:** Identity theft and related themes can touch upon sensitive topics such as personal privacy, security, and trust. Approach these themes with sensitivity and empathy, taking care not to trivialize or sensationalize the real-world consequences of identity theft. It's important to strike a balance between dramatic tension and respectful treatment of the issues at hand, particularly if the story involves characters who have experienced identity theft firsthand.

3. **Avoid Excessive Reliance on Plot Conveniences:** While the Stolen Identity trope can introduce compelling narrative twists,

avoid relying too heavily on contrived plot conveniences or unlikely coincidences to drive the story forward. Instead, plot developments should arise organically from the characters' choices, motivations, and conflicts. By grounding the narrative in believable human behavior, you can create a more immersive reading experience that connects with audiences.

Incorporating the Stolen Identity trope into a novel can inject intrigue and suspense into the narrative, but it also requires careful handling to avoid common pitfalls. By maintaining consistency and believability, handling sensitive themes with care, and avoiding excessive reliance on plot conveniences, you can effectively harness the power of this trope to craft engaging and compelling mysteries that captivate readers from start to finish.

Examples of the Stolen Identity Trope

Characters find themselves entangled in a web of deception and intrigue as they grapple with the repercussions of having their identity stolen in the Stolen Identity trope. From mistaken identities to malicious impersonations, these stories delve into the complexities of self-discovery and the quest for truth amidst a world of lies. Following are a few exceptions:

- In *The Bourne Identity* by Robert Ludlum, Jason Bourne, a man suffering from amnesia, discovers he is a highly trained assassin with a stolen identity. As Bourne unravels the mystery of his past, he must confront his former handlers and uncover the truth behind his stolen identity before they eliminate him for good.

- In *Alias Grace* by Margaret Atwood, Grace Marks is accused of murder but claims to have no memory of the crime. As the investigation unfolds, it becomes clear Grace's identity is not as straightforward as it seems, leading to a complex and gripping exploration of memory, guilt, and the nature of truth.

- Yakov Golyadkin is a government clerk who discovers his exact double has stolen his identity and is intent on ruining his life, in *The Double* by Fyodor Dostoevsky. The Stolen Identity trope is used to explore themes of paranoia and existential crisis as Golyadkin descends into madness trying to reclaim his sense of self.

The Stolen Identity trope adds depth and complexity, inviting readers into a world where identities are fluid and the truth is elusive.

Time Travel Trope
(HM, OM, PM)

Time Travel Trope Overview

The Time Travel trope is a fascinating narrative device often employed in science fiction and fantasy genres, allowing characters to journey backward or forward in time. It introduces an element of unpredictability and exploration as characters navigate through different historical periods or potential futures. This trope can be used to explore profound philosophical questions about fate, causality, and the nature of existence. Characters may attempt to alter past events to change the course of history or prevent future catastrophes, leading to moral dilemmas and unintended consequences. Time travel stories often feature intricate plots with multiple timelines, paradoxes, and alternate realities, challenging both characters and readers to unravel the complexities of temporal manipulation. Overall, the Time Travel trope offers a captivating blend of adventure, speculation, and intellectual inquiry, inviting audiences to ponder the mysteries of time itself.

The Time Travel trope, while primarily associated with science fiction, can also find its place within mystery narratives, adding layers of complexity and intrigue to the storyline. It is most commonly found in sub-genres that allow for speculative elements or unconventional narrative structures.

In historical mystery, time travel can feature prominently in the narratives, where protagonists may find themselves transported back in time to investigate crimes or uncover secrets from the past. This sub-genre allows you to weave together elements of historical fiction and mystery, offering readers a glimpse into different time periods while unraveling compelling mysteries rooted in the past.

Within the paranormal mystery and occult mystery sub-genres, the Time Travel trope may manifest in supernatural phenomena or magical artifacts that enable characters to transcend time. Protagonists may encounter ghosts, spirits, or mystical objects with the power to manipulate time, leading them on mysterious journeys across different temporal planes as they unravel enigmatic puzzles and confront ancient mysteries.

Overall, the Time Travel trope can add a unique dimension to mystery narratives, allowing you to explore themes of causality, consequence, and the fluidity of time itself. This trope offers endless possibilities for inventive storytelling and captivating plot twists.

Why Readers Love the Time Travel Trope

Readers love the Time Travel trope for its captivating ability to transport them across temporal boundaries and immerse them in richly imagined worlds both past and future. At its core, time travel taps into a fundamental curiosity about what lies beyond the constraints of the present moment, inviting readers on exhilarating journeys through history, alternate realities, and speculative futures. This trope offers a tantalizing escape from the mundane confines of everyday life, allowing readers to explore distant epochs, witness pivotal historical events, and ponder the tantalizing possibilities of what might lie ahead.

One of the key appeals of the Time Travel trope is its capacity to fuel imaginative speculation and thought-provoking exploration of the ramifications of altering the past or shaping the future. Readers are fascinated by the ethical dilemmas, paradoxes, and moral quandaries inherent in time travel narratives, which compel them to ponder questions about fate, free will, and the nature of causality. The element of unpredictability and the potential for unforeseen consequences keep readers holding their breath, eagerly anticipating each twist and turn as characters navigate the temporal landscape.

This trope allows readers to experience history in a deeply personal and immersive way, forging emotional connections with characters who traverse the ages and witness epochal events firsthand. Whether exploring the ancient world, reliving pivotal moments in human history, or venturing into speculative futures, readers are captivated by the opportunity to gain new perspectives on familiar narratives and to contemplate the enduring mysteries of the human experience across time and space. In essence, the Time Travel trope serves as a gateway to boundless realms of imagination, inviting readers to embark on thrilling odysseys through the annals of time.

What to Watch for When Using the Time Travel Trope

When employing the Time Travel trope in your novels, you will need to navigate various challenges to ensure a coherent and engaging narrative. While this trope offers immense creative potential, it also presents pitfalls to be wary of to maintain narrative cohesion and reader engagement. These include:

1. **Consistency in Time Travel Mechanics:** Establish clear rules and mechanics governing time travel within your story world. Inconsistencies or contradictions in how time travel operates can confuse readers and undermine the credibility of the narrative. It's essential to establish parameters such as the method of time travel, its limitations, and the consequences of altering the timeline, and then adhere to these rules consistently throughout the story.

2. **Managing Exposition and Backstory:** Time travel narratives often require extensive exposition to establish the rules of the world and provide necessary backstory. However, excessive exposition can bog down the pacing and detract from the momentum of the story. Skillfully integrate explanations of time travel mechanics and historical context into the narrative, balancing information with action and character development to maintain reader interest.

3. **Addressing Paradoxes and Logical Inconsistencies:** The nature of time travel inherently introduces paradoxes and logical inconsistencies that can be challenging to resolve. Carefully consider the implications of temporal manipulation and anticipate potential paradoxes within your narrative. While some degree of suspension of disbelief is necessary, strive to minimize illogical plot holes and guarantee the story's internal logic remains coherent and internally consistent.

Incorporating the Time Travel trope into a novel offers you boundless opportunities for creativity and exploration. However, to effectively leverage this trope and captivate readers, you must navigate potential pitfalls such as consistency in time travel mechanics, managing exposition, and addressing paradoxes. By carefully crafting your narratives with attention to these considerations, you can create immersive and compelling stories that transport readers on thrilling journeys through time.

Examples of the Time Travel Trope

The Time Travel trope is a fascinating element where characters find themselves navigating the complexities of time and space to solve enigmatic puzzles and unravel mysteries spanning across different eras. From altering the course of history to uncovering hidden secrets of the past, these stories offer readers a captivating blend of science fiction and detective intrigue. Here are six examples of mystery genre books that ingeniously incorporate the Time Travel trope to captivate readers with tales of suspense and temporal adventure.

- In *Time and Again* by Jack Finney, illustrator Si Morley participates in a secret government experiment that sends him back in time to New York City in the late 19th century. The Time Travel trope is used to immerse readers in the rich historical setting as Si investigates a mystery involving a beautiful woman and a tragic murder.

- In *The Shining Girls* by Lauren Beukes, a time-traveling serial killer stalks his victims across different decades, leaving behind no trace except for a mysterious token. The Time Travel trope adds a unique twist to the traditional murder mystery as the protagonist, Kirby Mazrachi, hunts down her would-be killer across time, determined to stop him before he strikes again.

- *The Map of Time* by Félix J. Palma intertwines multiple narratives set in Victorian London, where characters encounter time travel and its consequences. As the characters' paths intersect and diverge across time, they become entangled in a web of secrets and intrigue, leading to a thrilling and suspenseful exploration of fate, love, and the nature of reality.

The Time Travel trope offers mystery genre books a unique and intriguing premise, allowing authors to explore themes of destiny, consequence, and the human condition across the fabric of time itself. These six examples demonstrate the versatility of the trope, captivating readers with tales of temporal adventure and suspense that transcend the boundaries of conventional mystery fiction.

Twist Ending Trope
(HBM, HCM, NM, PT, STM)

The Twist Ending trope is a narrative device used in storytelling where the plot takes an unexpected turn or reveals a surprising revelation in the final moments of the story. This twist often subverts the audience's expectations and challenges their assumptions about the characters, events, or underlying themes of the narrative. Twist endings can range from shocking revelations about a character's true identity to unexpected plot developments that completely alter the trajectory of the story. When executed effectively, a twist ending can leave a lasting impression on the audience, prompting them to reconsider everything they thought they knew about the story and prompting them to reflect on its deeper meaning. However, twist endings must be carefully crafted to feel earned and satisfying, avoiding the pitfalls of being overly contrived or manipulative. Ultimately, the Twist Ending trope adds an element of unpredictability and intrigue to the narrative, keeping audiences engaged and eager to see how the story unfolds until the very end.

The Twist Ending trope is a versatile narrative device that can be found across various mystery sub-genres, adding intrigue and surprise to the resolution of the story. One of the most common sub-genres where the

Twist Ending trope is prevalent is the psychological thriller. In these stories, the twist often involves a revelation about the protagonist's mental state or the true nature of their reality, leaving readers questioning their perceptions and assumptions.

Another sub-genre where the Twist Ending trope frequently appears is the suspense thriller mystery. These novels typically build tension throughout the narrative, leading readers to anticipate a climactic revelation or unexpected turn of events. The twist ending in these stories often involves a shocking revelation about the identity of the antagonist or the true motives behind their actions, leaving readers reeling with surprise.

Additionally, the Twist Ending trope is commonly found in the hard-boiled mystery sub-genre, where it serves to subvert readers' expectations and challenge their assumptions about the resolution of the mystery. Whether it's a sudden reversal of fortune for the protagonist or a shocking revelation about the true culprit, the twist ending in these stories keeps readers captivated by your narrative until the very end.

By delivering unexpected revelations and surprising plot twists, this trope adds depth and intrigue to the story, keeping readers engaged and eager to uncover the truth until the very last page.

Why Readers Love the Twist Ending Trope

Readers love the Twist Ending trope because it provides them with a sense of satisfaction and surprise, enhancing their overall reading experience. The Twist Ending subverts expectations and adds an element of unpredictability to the narrative. This unpredictability keeps readers engaged and invested in the story, as they are constantly trying to anticipate what will happen next. A well-executed twist ending can challenge readers' assumptions and force them to reevaluate the events of the story from a new perspective. This intellectual stimulation adds depth to the reading experience and encourages readers to critically analyze the plot and characters.

The Twist Ending often delivers a satisfying payoff by resolving key plot points in unexpected ways. This resolution can tie up loose ends, answer lingering questions, and provide closure for readers. Additionally, the twist ending can prompt strong emotional reactions from readers, such as shock, awe, or even admiration for the author's creativity and ingenuity. These emotional responses create a memorable reading experience that resonates with readers long after they've finished the book.

The Twist Ending trope has become a hallmark of many beloved mystery novels, contributing to their popularity and enduring appeal. Readers are drawn to these genres precisely because they enjoy the challenge of unraveling complex plots and solving intricate puzzles. The twist ending adds an extra layer of complexity to these puzzles, providing readers with a satisfying payoff for their intellectual investment in the story. Overall, readers love the twist ending trope because it keeps them guessing, surprises them with unexpected revelations, and ultimately delivers a memorable and fulfilling reading experience.

What to Watch for When Using the Twist Ending Trope

When incorporating the Twist Ending trope into your novels, be mindful of the following items to guarantee the twist enhances rather than detracts from the overall narrative. These items include:

1. **Premature Revelation:** Avoid revealing the twist too early in the story, as this can diminish its impact. A well-executed twist should come as a surprise to readers, so it's crucial to maintain suspense and build anticipation leading up to the reveal.

2. **Lack of Foreshadowing:** A twist ending should feel both surprising and inevitable in retrospect. To achieve this balance, you must incorporate subtle clues and foreshadowing throughout the narrative to hint at the twist without giving it away entirely. Without adequate foreshadowing, the twist may feel contrived or disconnected from the rest of the story.

3. **Disregarding Character Development:** The twist ending should be rooted in the characters' motivations, actions, and relationships established throughout the story. Be certain the twist is consistent with the characters' personalities and behaviors, avoiding plot twists that feel forced or out of character.

4. **Unrealistic Resolution:** While a twist ending can defy readers' expectations, it should still be plausible within the context of the story's world and internal logic. Try for a balance between surprise and believability, avoiding twists that rely on improbable coincidences or deus ex machina resolutions.

5. **Neglecting Reader Satisfaction:** Ultimately, the twist ending should leave readers feeling satisfied rather than cheated or confused. Consider how the twist impacts the story's themes, resolution, and emotional payoff for readers. A well-executed twist should provide a sense of closure while leaving room for interpretation and discussion.

When executed thoughtfully and skillfully, a twist ending can elevate a novel and contribute to its enduring appeal.

Examples of the Twist Ending Trope

The Twist Ending trope offers readers unexpected plot twists and revelations that upend their assumptions and keep them guessing until the very last page. From shocking reveals to clever deceptions, these stories captivate audiences with their clever storytelling and narrative sleight of hand. Here are examples of mystery genre books that incorporate the Twist Ending trope to deliver unforgettable and satisfying conclusions.

- In *Gone Girl* by Gillian Flynn, the disappearance of Amy Dunne leads to a gripping investigation that takes unexpected turns as secrets are unearthed and lies are exposed. The Twist Ending trope is utilized as Flynn subverts readers' expectations with a shocking reveal that changes everything they thought they knew about the characters and their motivations.

- Agatha Christie is a master of the twist ending. *The Murder of Roger Ackroyd* is a classic example of the Twist Ending trope, featuring Hercule Poirot's investigation into the murder of a wealthy industrialist. As Poirot unravels the mystery, he uncovers a startling twist that challenges everything the reader thought they knew about the case and the identity of the killer.

- In Christie's, *And Then There Were None* it follows ten strangers who are lured to a remote island where they are killed off one by one. The Twist Ending trope is used to perfection as Christie delivers a stunning conclusion that completely subverts readers' expectations and leaves them reeling with its cleverness and audacity.

The Twist Ending trope offers readers thrilling and unexpected conclusions that linger long after the final page. It enables clever storytelling and surprising reveals that keep readers guessing until the very end.

Undercover Investigations Trope (LT, PP)

The Undercover Investigations trope is a classic narrative device employed in mystery and thriller genres to create suspenseful and thrilling plotlines. It involves characters assuming false identities and infiltrating criminal organizations, corrupt institutions, or secretive groups to gather information or thwart nefarious schemes. Undercover operatives often face perilous situations as they navigate the delicate balance between maintaining their cover and uncovering the truth. This trope offers opportunities for intense psychological drama, as characters grapple with the moral complexities of their dual identities and the ethical dilemmas of their missions. Themes of loyalty, betrayal, and redemption are common, as undercover agents must confront their own principles and motivations amidst the dangerous underworld they inhabit. Ultimately, the Undercover Investigations trope adds layers of intrigue and suspense to narratives, keeping audiences on the edge of their seats as they unravel the mysteries hidden beneath the surface.

The Undercover Investigations trope is a staple of various mystery sub-genres. In legal thrillers, undercover investigations are frequently employed by detectives or private investigators to infiltrate criminal organizations or gather evidence on suspects. These stories often delve into the complexities of undercover work, exploring the ethical dilemmas faced by protagonists as they navigate dual identities and blurred moral lines.

In police procedurals, the Undercover Investigations trope is often employed by law enforcement officers seeking to gather intelligence on criminal activities or uncover corruption within their ranks. These stories showcase the challenges of undercover work within the context of police investigations, highlighting the risks and rewards of going undercover to solve crimes. The trope adds depth to procedural narratives, allowing for exploration of themes such as trust, loyalty, and the blurred boundaries between law enforcement and criminality.

Whether exploring the seedy underbelly of criminal enterprises, unraveling international espionage plots, or uncovering corruption within law enforcement agencies, the trope offers endless opportunities for tension, intrigue, and unexpected twists.

Why Readers Love the Undercover Investigations Trope

Readers are drawn to the Undercover Investigations trope for its ability to immerse them in the thrilling world of deception, intrigue, and suspense. At its core, this trope offers a tantalizing glimpse into the clandestine operations of undercover agents, detectives, or spies as they navigate dangerous situations and assume false identities to achieve their objectives. The element of secrecy and the constant threat of discovery keep readers on pins and needles, eagerly turning pages to uncover the truth behind the elaborate ruses and hidden agendas.

This trope allows readers to experience a sense of vicarious thrill as they accompany protagonists on perilous missions into the heart of criminal organizations, terrorist cells, or corrupt institutions. The tension inherent in maintaining a cover identity while infiltrating hostile environments creates a palpable atmosphere of suspense, keeping readers engaged and invested in the outcome of the investigation. Whether it's a gritty crime novel, a pulse-pounding espionage thriller, or a gripping police procedural, the allure of the undercover operation lies in its ability to transport readers into the murky underworld of covert operations.

The complexity of the characters involved in undercover investigations adds another layer of appeal for readers. Protagonists tasked with going undercover often grapple with moral dilemmas, ethical compromises, and internal conflicts as they navigate the murky waters of deception and betrayal. These multidimensional characters undergo profound transformations as they confront their own vulnerabilities and question their allegiances, making for compelling narrative arcs that strikes a chord with readers on a deeper level.

Ultimately, the Undercover Investigations trope captivates readers by offering a tantalizing blend of suspense, intrigue, and moral ambiguity. Whether it's the adrenaline-fueled action of a spy thriller, the gritty realism of a crime novel, or the meticulous procedural detail of a police investigation, the allure of going undercover lies in its ability to transport readers into a world of danger, deception, and unexpected revelations.

What to Watch for When Using the Undercover Investigations Trope

When employing the Undercover Investigations trope in your novels, be mindful of several key considerations to ensure its effective execution. This trope, while inherently captivating, comes with its own set of challenges and pitfalls you must navigate skillfully to maintain authenticity and reader engagement.

1. **Establishing Plausible Cover Identities:** The cover identities assumed by your characters must be credible and well-developed. Readers are quick to pick up on inconsistencies or unrealistic portrayals, so you must invest time in crafting cover stories that align with the character's background, skills, and motivations.

2. **Balancing Suspense and Realism:** While the undercover operation should be fraught with tension and suspense, you must strike a balance between dramatic flair and realism. Overly contrived scenarios or improbable twists can strain believability and undermine the narrative's credibility. It's essential to ground the story in a plausible framework while still delivering the requisite thrills and twists.

3. **Managing Character Conflicts and Moral Dilemmas:** Characters involved in undercover investigations often grapple with ethical dilemmas, conflicting loyalties, and internal struggles. Explore these complexities in a nuanced manner, allowing characters to wrestle with their conscience and navigate the moral gray areas inherent in undercover work. However, care must be taken to avoid clichéd or overly melodramatic portrayals of inner conflict.

4. **Researching Law Enforcement Procedures:** Conduct thorough research into law enforcement protocols, investigative techniques, and procedural details relevant to undercover operations. Accuracy in depicting police procedures and legal

constraints adds depth and authenticity to the narrative, enhancing the reader's immersion in the story.

5. **Avoiding Stereotypes and Tropes:** While the Undercover Investigations trope is a staple of the mystery genre, try to avoid clichés and stereotypes commonly associated with undercover agents or covert operations. Instead, endeavor to create unique and multidimensional characters who defy conventional expectations and offer fresh perspectives on the genre.

By paying heed to these considerations and approaching the trope with creativity and authenticity, you can craft compelling narratives that captivate readers and keep them guessing until the final revelation.

Examples of the Undercover Investigations Trope

The Undercover Investigations trope adds an element of suspense and intrigue as protagonists immerse themselves in dangerous situations to uncover the truth from within. From infiltrating criminal organizations to assuming false identities, these stories captivate readers with your tension-filled narratives and high-stakes undercover operations. Here are som examples:

- In *The Girl with the Dragon Tattoo* by Stieg Larsson, journalist Mikael Blomkvist and hacker Lisbeth Salander delve into the dark underbelly of Swedish society, conducting undercover investigations to expose corruption and violence. Blomkvist and Salander assume false identities and risk their lives to uncover the truth behind a decades-old disappearance.

- *Undercover* by Danielle Steel follows Marshall Everett, an undercover agent tasked with infiltrating a dangerous criminal syndicate. As Marshall immerses himself in the criminal underworld, he must navigate a treacherous web of deceit and betrayal, risking everything to bring down the organization from within.

- *The Poet* by Michael Connelly follows journalist Jack McEvoy as he goes undercover to investigate a series of murders committed by a cunning serial killer. The Undercover Investigations trope drives the novel's plot as McEvoy risks his life to expose the killer's identity, leading to a tense and suspenseful showdown with deadly consequences.

The Undercover Investigations trope adds depth and suspense, immersing readers in the thrilling world of undercover operations and high-stakes investigations. These examples demonstrate the versatility and impact of the trope, offering gripping and suspenseful tales of deception, danger, and intrigue.

Unreliable Narrator Trope
(HM, NM, LT, PM, PT, SKM)

Unreliable Narrator Trope Overview

The Unreliable Narrator trope is a narrative technique where the credibility and trustworthiness of the narrator's perspective are called into question, either intentionally or unintentionally. This device creates ambiguity and uncertainty for the reader, as they must navigate conflicting or questionable information presented by the narrator. Unreliable narrators may distort facts, omit crucial details, or provide biased interpretations of events, leading to an unreliable portrayal of the story's events and characters. This trope is commonly used in mystery, thriller, and psychological fiction genres to add complexity, intrigue, and suspense to the narrative. It challenges readers to critically analyze the story and consider multiple perspectives, often revealing deeper layers of meaning and truth beneath the surface. Ultimately, the Unreliable Narrator trope invites readers to question the nature of storytelling itself, highlighting the subjective nature of perception and interpretation in shaping narrative truth.

The Unreliable Narrator trope is found in a variety of mystery sub-genres, where it adds layers of intrigue, ambiguity, and suspense to the storytelling. One sub-genre where the Unreliable Narrator is frequently employed is psychological thrillers. In these stories, the protagonist's perception of reality is often called into question, blurring the lines between truth and deception. This creates a sense of unease and uncertainty for both the protagonist and the reader, as they navigate a narrative landscape rife with hidden agendas and unreliable perspectives.

In noir mysteries, the narrator may withhold or distort information about their relationships, family dynamics, or personal histories. This leads to twists and revelations that challenge the readers' perceptions of the characters and their motivations. This sub-genre often features morally ambiguous characters and complex narrative structures where the unreliable narrator may be involved in criminal activities, deception, or manipulation. This blurs the line between truth and deception.

The Unreliable Narrator trope also finds its way at times into the paranormal mysteries, historical mysteries, legal thrillers, and serial killer thrillers sub-genres. In paranormal mysteries, the protagonist often experiences supernatural phenomena or encounter otherworldly beings. This leads to uncertainty about the reliability of their perceptions and interpretations of events, making them an unreliable narrator. In historical mysteries, the unreliable narrator can be used to depict characters navigating the complexities of historical events, political intrigue, or societal norms, with perspectives that are shaped by bias, prejudice, or limited information.

In contrast, legal thrillers may use the Unreliable Narrator trope may be lawyers, defendants, or witnesses involved in courtroom dramas, where conflicting accounts of events and unreliable testimony create suspense and uncertainty. And these unreliable narrators may expand to include detectives, journalists or even survivors in the serial killer thrill sub-genre, where their motivations are clouded by trauma, obsession, or personal agendas.

Why Readers Love the Unreliable Narrator Trope

The Unreliable Narrator trope is a reader favorite for its ability to subvert expectations and challenge their perceptions of reality. The unreliable narrator introduces an element of mystery and suspense into the narrative, keeping readers engaged as they attempt to unravel the truth hidden beneath layers of deception. This uncertainty adds an extra layer of complexity to the storytelling, inviting readers to actively participate in piecing together the puzzle of the narrative.

Additionally, the Unreliable Narrator trope allows authors to explore themes of memory, perception, and subjective truth in compelling ways. By presenting events through the lens of an unreliable narrator, authors can delve into the intricacies of human psychology and the fallibility of memory, raising thought-provoking questions about the nature of truth and reality. This intellectual challenge appeals to readers who enjoy narratives that encourage them to critically analyze and interpret the story's events.

It adds an element of suspense and tension to the narrative, as readers are kept on edge, never quite sure whether they can trust the narrator's version of events. This heightened sense of uncertainty creates a page-turning experience, as readers eagerly anticipate the next revelation or plot twist that may shed light on the true nature of the story. Ultimately, it is this sense of anticipation and suspense that keeps readers engaged and invested in the narrative, making the Unreliable Narrator trope a popular choice among fans of mystery and psychological fiction.

What to Watch for When Using the Unreliable Narrator Trope

Using the Unreliable Narrator trope can add depth and complexity to a story, but it's one of the more difficult tropes to use properly. Paying attention to the items below can help you use the Unreliable Narrator effectively.

1. **Overuse:** While the Unreliable Narrator trope can be effective in creating suspense and intrigue, using it too frequently or gratuitously can confuse readers and detract from the overall impact of the narrative.

2. **Lack of Clarity:** It's essential to strike a balance between ambiguity and clarity when employing an unreliable narrator. If readers become too frustrated or confused by the narrator's unreliability, they may disengage from the story altogether.

3. **Unrealistic Characterization:** The unreliable narrator should be believable within the context of the story. You must be sure the narrator's motivations and behavior are consistent with their established character traits, avoiding abrupt shifts that strain credibility.

4. **Failing to Provide Clues:** While the unreliability of the narrator may be revealed gradually over the course of the story, still provide subtle clues and foreshadowing to hint at the truth. Without sufficient groundwork, readers may feel cheated or manipulated when the truth is finally revealed.

5. **Neglecting Reader Trust:** Ultimately, readers need to trust the author is guiding them through the narrative in good faith. Be cautious not to abuse the reader's trust by employing the Unreliable Narrator trope solely for shock value or to manipulate emotions.

While the Unreliable Narrator trope can be a powerful tool for storytelling, you must approach it with care and consideration.

Examples of the Unreliable Narrator Trope

The Unreliable Narrator trope adds layers of ambiguity and intrigue to the narrative. These protagonists, whether intentionally or unintentionally, provide skewed or incomplete perspectives on the events unfolding, leading readers down paths of uncertainty and doubt. Here are some examples:

- *The Silent Patient* by Alex Michaelides follows psychotherapist Theo Faber as he attempts to unravel the mystery of Alicia Berenson, a woman accused of murdering her husband who has remained silent ever since. The Unreliable Narrator trope is central to the novel as Alicia's silence and Theo's own motivations cast doubt on the reliability of the narrative, leading to a suspenseful and psychologically gripping exploration of guilt and madness.

- *Sharp Objects* by Gillian Flynn features journalist Camille Preaker, whose troubled past and history of self-harm make her an unreliable narrator as she investigates a series of murders in her hometown. Flynn uses the Unreliable Narrator trope to immerse readers in Camille's fractured psyche, blurring the lines between reality and hallucination as she delves deeper into the dark secrets of her past.

- In *The Tell-Tale Heart* by Edgar Allan Poe, the unnamed narrator's descent into madness and obsession with an old man's "vulture eye" creates an atmosphere of unreliability and suspense. Poe masterfully employs the Unreliable Narrator trope to draw readers into the narrator's twisted mind, leading to a chilling and haunting exploration of guilt and paranoia.

The Unreliable Narrator trope is a captivating element that offers readers a lens through which to explore the complexities of truth and perception. The versatility and impact of the trope immerses readers in tales of psychological suspense and moral ambiguity that challenge their perceptions and keep them guessing until the final revelation.

Unsolved Mysteries Trope
(CM, PP, PT, STM)

Unsolved Mysteries Trope Overview

The Unsolved Mysteries trope is a captivating narrative device frequently employed in mystery and suspense genres to keep audiences engaged and intrigued. It revolves around enigmatic and perplexing cases, crimes, or phenomena that defy conventional explanation or resolution. These mysteries often involve baffling clues, elusive suspects, or supernatural elements, adding an air of suspense and intrigue to the storyline. Characters, whether amateur sleuths, detectives, or ordinary individuals, become embroiled in the quest to unravel these puzzles, driven by curiosity, justice, or personal stakes. The trope allows storytellers to explore themes of uncertainty, human nature, and the unknown, as well as to challenge conventional notions of truth and reality. With its inherent sense of suspense and unanswered questions, the Unsolved Mysteries trope captivates audiences by inviting them to participate in the investigation and speculate on possible outcomes, keeping them eagerly turning pages or glued to the screen until the final revelation.

Why Readers Love the Unsolved Mysteries Trope

The Unsolved Mysteries trope is a versatile narrative device that can be found across various mystery sub-genres, each offering its own unique spin on unresolved enigmas and puzzling conundrums. In the realm of traditional detective fiction, this trope often manifests in the form of cold cases or unsolved murders that continue to haunt investigators and protagonists long after the initial crime. In police procedurals, unsolved mysteries may serve as recurring plot threads, driving ongoing investigations and providing a backdrop of intrigue and suspense.

Similarly, in psychological thrillers and suspense thriller mystery novels, the Unsolved Mysteries trope may take on a more psychological dimension, with characters grappling with elusive truths, buried secrets, and unresolved traumas from their past. These mysteries may be deeply intertwined with the protagonist's psyche, fueling a sense of unease and existential dread as they navigate a labyrinth of hidden truths and half-forgotten memories. In supernatural or paranormal mysteries, the trope may manifest in unexplained phenomena, occult mysteries, or paranormal events that defy rational explanation.

The Unsolved Mysteries trope can also be a central theme in cozy mysteries, where amateur sleuths or eccentric detectives set out to unravel perplexing puzzles and solve seemingly unsolvable crimes in quaint and idyllic settings. These stories often feature a cast of quirky characters, red herrings, and unexpected twists, adding layers of complexity to the overarching mystery. Regardless of the sub-genre, the Unsolved Mysteries trope captivates readers with its sense of intrigue, suspense, and the tantalizing promise of uncovering hidden truths lurking beneath the surface.

What to Watch for When Using the Unsolved Mysteries Trope

Introducing the Unsolved Mysteries trope into a novel can add layers of intrigue and suspense, but navigate this narrative device with caution to guarantee its effectiveness and avoid potential pitfalls. Here are some considerations to keep in mind when incorporating unsolved mysteries into your story:

1. **Establish Clear Resolution Expectations:** Be mindful of reader expectations regarding the resolution of unsolved mysteries. While leaving some elements open-ended can add to the story's mystique, ensure readers are not left feeling unsatisfied or frustrated by a lack of closure.

2. **Maintain Narrative Coherence:** Avoid introducing too many unresolved plot threads or mysteries that distract from the central narrative. Each unsolved mystery should serve a purpose in advancing the plot or developing characters, rather than merely serving as a narrative device without payoff.

3. **Balance Clues and Red Herrings:** Strive for a balance between providing clues that lead readers toward potential resolutions and introducing red herrings that keep them guessing. Too many false leads or insufficient clues can undermine the reader's engagement and make the resolution feel arbitrary or unsatisfying.

4. **Avoid Clichés and Predictability:** While unsolved mysteries can be compelling, be wary of falling into clichés or predictable tropes. Surprise readers with unexpected twists and revelations that

challenge their assumptions and keep them engaged in the unraveling of the mystery.

5. **Develop Compelling Characters:** Your characters involved in the investigation of unsolved mysteries must be well-developed and multidimensional. Readers should be invested in their journeys and motivations, rooting for their success in solving the mysteries and uncovering the truth.

While the Unsolved Mysteries trope can add depth and intrigue to a novel, you must approach it thoughtfully to maintain reader engagement and satisfaction. By establishing clear resolution expectations, maintaining narrative coherence, balancing clues and red herrings, avoiding clichés, and developing compelling characters, you can effectively leverage this trope to captivate readers and keep them guessing until the very end.

Examples of the Unsolved Mysteries Trope

The Unsolved Mysteries trope features enigmatic puzzles and unresolved questions that linger long after the final page. From cold cases to unexplained phenomena, these stories immerse readers in tales of intrigue and suspense as protagonists grapple with the elusive nature of truth. Here are a few examples of novels that skillfully incorporate the Unsolved Mysteries trope to keep readers on the edge of anticipation.

- *The Hound of the Baskervilles* by Arthur Conan Doyle follows Sherlock Holmes and Dr. John Watson as they investigate the mysterious death of Sir Charles Baskerville, allegedly caused by a supernatural hound. The Unsolved Mysteries trope is central to the novel as Holmes and Watson navigate the fog-shrouded moors of Dartmoor, unraveling a web of secrets and deception to uncover the truth behind the ancient curse that haunts the Baskerville family.

- In *In the Woods* by Tana French, detective Rob Ryan investigates the murder of a young girl in a small Irish town, a case eerily reminiscent of his own childhood trauma. The Unsolved Mysteries trope is utilized to great effect as Ryan grapples with his own buried memories and the lingering questions surrounding the disappearance of his two childhood friends, leading to a suspenseful and emotionally resonant investigation.

- In *The Da Vinci Code* by Dan Brown, symbologist Robert Langdon and cryptologist Sophie Neveu race against time to unravel a centuries-old conspiracy involving the Catholic Church and the secret of the Holy Grail. The unsolved mystery of what happened to the Holy Grail is central to the novel as Langdon and Neveu follow a trail of cryptic clues and hidden messages, uncovering a web of deceit and intrigue that stretches across time and space.

- *The Shadow of the Wind* by Carlos Ruiz Zafón is set in post-war Barcelona, where a young boy discovers a mysterious book that leads him on a quest to uncover the truth behind its enigmatic author and the dark secrets of his past. The Unsolved Mysteries trope is intricately woven into the novel's labyrinthine plot as the protagonist delves deeper into the shadowy underworld of literature and intrigue, leading to a mesmerizing and haunting tale of love, betrayal, and redemption.

The Unsolved Mysteries trope draws readers into tales of intrigue, suspense, and moral ambiguity. The trope, offers gripping and suspenseful narratives that leave readers questioning the nature of truth and the mysteries that lie beneath the surface.

Witness Protection Trope
(LT, PP, STM)

Witness Protection Trope Overview

The Witness Protection trope is a plot device commonly used in mystery and crime fiction to protect individuals who have provided crucial testimony or evidence in criminal cases. Typically, witnesses are relocated and provided with new identities to shield them from retaliation by criminal organizations or individuals seeking retribution. This trope often involves elaborate schemes orchestrated by law enforcement agencies to safeguard witnesses and their families, including changing their appearance, residence, and even their occupations. As part of the witness protection program, strict protocols are enforced to maintain secrecy and prevent the disclosure of the witness's new identity. However, the inherent risks and challenges of living under a new identity, as well as the constant fear of discovery, create tension and suspense in stories featuring this trope. Additionally, the theme of redemption and second chances is often explored as witnesses grapple with the repercussions of their past and strive to build new lives free from danger and fear.

The Witness Protection trope is most commonly found in mystery sub-genres that involve crime, law enforcement, and legal proceedings. One prevalent sub-genre where this trope often appears is the police procedural, where law enforcement officers work to protect witnesses and gather evidence to solve crimes. In these narratives, witnesses may play a crucial role in unraveling complex cases, often requiring them to be placed under protective custody to be certain their safety.

Another sub-genre where the Witness Protection trope frequently features is the legal thriller, where attorneys and legal professionals navigate the complexities of the justice system to defend their clients or prosecute suspects. In these stories, witnesses may hold key information or provide crucial testimony, making their protection vital to the outcome of legal proceedings. Witness protection may also be a central plot element in courtroom dramas, adding layers of tension and suspense to the narrative.

The Witness Protection trope can also appear in suspense thriller mystery sub-genres, particularly those involving organized crime, espionage, or government conspiracy. In these narratives, witnesses who possess incriminating evidence or insider knowledge may become targets for elimination by powerful adversaries. Placing witnesses under protection becomes a matter of life and death, as they must evade detection and navigate a shadowy world of danger and intrigue.

This trope adds an element of suspense and intrigue to mystery narratives by introducing characters whose lives are in peril due to their knowledge of criminal activities or involvement in high-stakes legal proceedings. By exploring themes of danger, betrayal, and redemption, you can create compelling stories that keep readers spellbound by the unfolding events until the final revelation.

Why Readers Love the Witness Protection Trope

The Witness Protection trope captivates readers for its ability to immerse them in a world of danger, intrigue, and suspense. At its core, this trope offers a thrilling narrative premise: ordinary individuals thrust into extraordinary circumstances, forced to leave behind their identities and start anew under the watchful eye of law enforcement. This premise taps into readers' fascination with the unknown and their desire to explore the complexities of human nature when faced with adversity.

It often presents readers with characters who are relatable and sympathetic, individuals whose lives are upended by events beyond their control. As readers follow these characters on their journey through secrecy and danger, they become emotionally invested in their struggles and triumphs, rooting for them to outwit their enemies and find a semblance of safety and normalcy in their new lives.

This trope offers the opportunity to explore themes of identity, trust, and resilience. By placing characters in situations where they must grapple with the loss of their former lives and forge new identities, you can delve into the psychological impact of trauma and the complexities of rebuilding one's sense of self in the face of adversity. This exploration of human resilience and the capacity for transformation stirs feelings with readers on a deep emotional level, drawing them further into the story.

Readers are drawn to the Witness Protection trope for its ability to deliver gripping narratives filled with suspense, intrigue, and emotional depth. Whether it's a gritty crime thriller or a heart-pounding legal drama, stories that feature characters navigating the perilous world of witness protection offer readers an immersive and thrilling reading experience that keeps them eagerly turning the pages until the very end.

What to Watch for When Using the Witness Protection Trope

Keep the following items in mind when incorporating the Witness Protection trope into your mystery:

1. **Authenticity**: Strive for authenticity when portraying the experience of individuals in witness protection. This includes researching the legal and procedural aspects of witness protection programs, as well as the emotional and psychological toll it takes on those involved.

2. **Character Development:** While the Witness Protection trope offers a compelling backdrop for storytelling, avoid relying solely on the premise to drive the narrative. It's essential to develop well-rounded characters with distinct personalities, motivations, and arcs to keep readers engaged and invested in their journey.

3. **Balancing Action and Emotion:** A successful novel featuring the Witness Protection trope strikes a balance between heart-pounding action and emotional depth. Make certain your story maintains tension and suspense while also exploring the emotional journey of your characters as they navigate the challenges of witness protection.

4. **Ethical Considerations:** Approach the portrayal of witness protection with sensitivity and respect for the real-world implications of the program. This includes considering the ethical implications of depicting law enforcement, criminals, and the impact of witness protection on individuals' lives.

Although the Witness Protection trope offers a rich and fertile ground for storytelling, it's essential to approach it with care and consideration. By focusing on authenticity, character development, originality, emotional depth, and ethical considerations, you can effectively harness the power of this trope to create engaging and thought-provoking narratives that resonate with readers.

Examples of the Witness Protection Trope

The Witness Protection trope adds a layer of intrigue and danger as protagonists are forced to assume new identities and navigate the complexities of life in hiding. From evading dangerous criminals to uncovering hidden truths, these stories captivate readers with your suspenseful narratives and high-stakes stakes. Here are some examples of how the trope delivers gripping tales of deception and survival.

- *The Innocent* by Harlan Coben follows Matt Hunter, a man who enters the Witness Protection Program after accidentally killing a man in a bar fight. Matt struggles to adapt to his new identity and uncover the truth behind the events that led to his life being turned upside down.

- In *The Witness* by Nora Roberts, a young woman named Elizabeth witnesses a brutal murder and is placed in the Witness Protection Program to secure her safety. Elizabeth grapples with the trauma of what she has seen while navigating the challenges of her new identity and forging a bond with the U.S. Marshal assigned to protect her.

- *Hideaway* by Nora Roberts follows a woman named Caitlyn Sullivan who goes into hiding after surviving a kidnapping attempt orchestrated by her stalker. The Witness Protection trope is used to heighten the tension and suspense as Caitlyn struggles to evade her would-be attacker while uncovering a web of secrets and lies that threaten to destroy her newfound sense of security.

The Witness Protection offers readers tales of danger, deception, and survival in the shadowy world of witness relocation. The trope, creates gripping narratives of suspense and intrigue.

Wrongful Conviction/Wrongly Accused Trope
(AS, CM, LT, PM, PP, PT)

Wrongful Conviction Trope Overview

The Wrongful Conviction trope is a compelling narrative device frequently employed in mystery and legal thriller genres. It revolves around the wrongful accusation and/or conviction of an individual for a crime they did not commit. Often rooted in flawed investigative procedures, biased testimonies, or fabricated evidence, the wrongful conviction serves as a catalyst for the protagonist's quest for justice. This trope explores themes of injustice, corruption, and the fallibility of the legal system, shining a light on the devastating consequences of miscarriages of justice. As the protagonist delves into the case, uncovering new evidence and challenging entrenched beliefs, they strive to exonerate the wrongfully convicted individual and expose the truth behind the crime. The Wrongful Conviction trope not only drives the plot forward but also raises important questions about the integrity of the criminal justice system and the need for reform to prevent future injustices.

The Wrongful Conviction trope is a recurring theme in various mystery sub-genres, often adding layers of complexity and moral ambiguity to the narrative. One sub-genre where this trope frequently appears is the legal thriller, where the focus is on courtroom drama and legal proceedings. In these stories, the protagonist, typically a defense attorney or an investigator, becomes embroiled in cases where individuals have been wrongly convicted of crimes they did not commit. The trope serves to highlight flaws in the justice system, such as police misconduct, prosecutorial bias, or inadequate legal representation, prompting the protagonist to uncover the truth and exonerate the wrongly accused.

The Wrongful Conviction trope is also prevalent in the sub-genre of police procedurals, where law enforcement officers investigate crimes and pursue suspects. In these stories, the trope often arises when police detectives or investigators realize they have arrested the wrong person based on faulty evidence, coerced confessions, or tunnel vision during the investigation. The narrative tension intensifies as the protagonist races against time to rectify the miscarriage of justice and bring the true perpetrator to light, grappling with institutional resistance and personal sacrifices along the way.

This trope can also feature prominently in the sub-genre of psychological thrillers, where the focus is on the intricate workings of the human mind and the motivations behind criminal behavior. In these stories, the protagonist may be a psychologist, forensic psychiatrist, or amateur sleuth who delves into the psychological complexities of a case to uncover the truth behind a wrongful conviction. The trope often challenges readers' perceptions of guilt and innocence, exploring themes of memory manipulation, gaslighting, and the fallibility of eyewitness testimony, while keeping them enthralled with the storyline with twists and turns.

In the amateur sleuth, cozy mystery, and paranormal mystery sub-genres, either the protagonist wrongfully accused of a crime or a friend or family member is usually how the protagonist gets involved in the case. This serves as the catalyst transforming the protagonist into an amateur sleuth wither the stakes in solving the crime are high. Whether set in the courtroom, the police station, or the depths of the human psyche, stories featuring this trope offer readers a compelling exploration of the human condition and the complexities of the justice system.

Why Readers Love the Wrongful Conviction Trope

Readers are drawn to the Wrongful Conviction trope for its compelling exploration of justice, morality, and the human condition. At its core, this trope taps into a deep-seated desire for fairness and truth, resonating with readers who value principles of equity and accountability in society. The idea of an innocent person being wrongfully convicted strikes a chord with readers' sense of empathy and compassion, evoking strong emotional responses as they witness the protagonist's struggle for exoneration and redemption.

This trope often serves as a catalyst for riveting storytelling, injecting suspense, drama, and moral ambiguity into the narrative. As readers follow the protagonist's journey to uncover the truth and overturn the wrongful conviction, they are swept along on a rollercoaster of twists, turns, and unexpected revelations. The trope creates a sense of urgency and tension, keeping readers completely absorbed by the narrative, as they eagerly anticipate the resolution of the protagonist's quest for justice.

The Wrongful Conviction trope invites readers to also reflect on broader societal issues surrounding the criminal justice system, such as systemic biases, flaws in legal procedures, and the impact of wrongful convictions on individuals and communities. By shining a spotlight on these themes, stories featuring this trope encourage readers to critically examine real-world injustices and advocate for reforms that guarantee fairness, accountability, and due process for all. Through thought-provoking narratives that challenge assumptions and highlight the complexities of the human experience, the Wrongful Conviction trope fosters empathy, understanding, and a deeper engagement with issues of social justice.

What to Watch for When Using the Wrongful Conviction Trope

Introducing the Wrongful Conviction trope into a novel can enrich the narrative with layers of complexity and moral dilemmas, but you must approach its use with caution to avoid common pitfalls. Here are some considerations to keep in mind when incorporating this trope:

1. **Establishing Realism:** Strive to portray the legal system accurately and realistically, avoiding overly simplistic or melodramatic portrayals of wrongful convictions. Researching legal procedures, forensic science, and the intricacies of criminal investigations can help maintain credibility and immerse readers in the story.

2. **Handling Sensitive Themes:** Wrongful convictions often involve themes of injustice, trauma, and loss, which can evoke strong emotional reactions in readers. You must approach these themes with sensitivity and empathy, avoiding gratuitous depictions of suffering or trauma. Providing nuanced portrayals of characters' experiences and emotions can foster deeper connections with readers.

3. **Balancing Pacing and Plotting:** While the quest for exoneration is central to many stories featuring the Wrongful

Conviction trope, you must be certain the pacing remains dynamic and the plot maintains momentum. Balancing the protagonist's pursuit of justice with other narrative elements, such as character development and subplot progression, can prevent the story from feeling stagnant or repetitive.

Although the Wrongful Conviction trope offers rich storytelling opportunities, you must navigate its complexities with care and thoughtfulness. By prioritizing realism, originality, sensitivity, and narrative balance, you can effectively harness the power of this trope to craft compelling and resonant narratives that captivate readers and provoke thought.

Examples of the Wrongful Conviction Trope

The Wrongfully Accused trope places protagonists in perilous situations as they struggle to clear their names and uncover the truth behind their unjust accusations. From navigating the complexities of the legal system to evading relentless pursuers, these stories captivate readers with your thrilling narratives and high-stakes stakes. Here are a few examples that deliver gripping tales of injustice and redemption.

- *The Fugitive* by David J. Schow follows Dr. Richard Kimble, who is wrongfully convicted of murdering his wife and goes on the run to prove his innocence. Kimble evades the relentless pursuit of the law while uncovering clues that point to the real killer, leading to a suspenseful and action-packed race against time.

- In *The Reversal* by Michael Connelly, defense attorney Mickey Haller takes on the case of a man who has spent twenty-four years in prison for a crime he didn't commit. Haller works tirelessly to exonerate his client and uncover the truth behind his wrongful conviction, leading to a riveting courtroom drama that challenges the limits of justice.

- *Presumed Innocent* by Scott Turow follows prosecutor Rusty Sabich, who is accused of murdering his colleague and former lover. Sabich navigates the complexities of the legal system while grappling with his own guilt and innocence, leading to a tense and suspenseful courtroom thriller that keeps readers guessing until the final verdict.

The Wrongfully Accused trope offers readers tales of injustice, redemption, and the triumph of the human spirit. The trope, provides gripping narratives of suspense and intrigue.

Character, Setting, & Genre Tropes Chart

SUB-GENRES: W = Whodunit · STM = Suspense Thriller Mystery · SKM = Serial Killer Mystery · PT = Psychological Thriller · PP = Police Procedural · PM = Paranormal Mystery · OM = Occult Mystery · NM = Noir Mystery · LT = Legal Thriller · HM = Historical Mystery · HCM = Heist and Caper Mystery · HBM = Hard-Boiled Mystery · GM = Gothic Mystery · FM = Forensic Mystery · CM = Cozy Mystery · AS = Amateur Sleuth

Trope	W	STM	SKM	PT	PP	PM	OM	NM	LT	HM	HCM	HBM	GM	FM	CM	AS	Category
Amateur Detective	✓					✓				✓					✓	✓	CHARACTER TROPES
Detective Duo					✓	✓									✓	✓	CHARACTER TROPES
Detective Protagonist			✓		✓							✓		✓	✓	✓	CHARACTER TROPES
Eccentric Detective					✓	✓						✓			✓	✓	CHARACTER TROPES
Femme Fatale				✓				✓	✓		✓		✓				CHARACTER TROPES
Hard-Boiled Detective		✓						✓				✓		✓			CHARACTER TROPES
Private Investigator	✓							✓				✓				✓	CHARACTER TROPES
Serial Killer			✓	✓	✓				✓								CHARACTER TROPES
Vigilante Detective		✓						✓				✓					CHARACTER TROPES
Haunted House						✓	✓						✓		✓		SETTING TROPES
Isolated Cabin	✓				✓												SETTING TROPES
Locked Room	✓									✓					✓		SETTING TROPES
Small Town	✓	✓		✓	✓	✓									✓	✓	SETTING TROPES
Urban Jungle		✓						✓						✓		✓	SETTING TROPES
Forensic Evidence					✓				✓					✓			GENRE TROPES
Legal Proceedings					✓				✓								GENRE TROPES
Noir Fiction				✓				✓				✓					GENRE TROPES
Police Procedural		✓	✓	✓					✓					✓			GENRE TROPES
Supernatural Mystery						✓	✓						✓		✓		GENRE TROPES
Whodunit	✓		✓	✓	✓						✓			✓	✓		GENRE TROPES

Plot Device Tropes Chart

Sub-genres (columns): Whodunit (W) · Suspense Thriller Mystery (STM) · Serial Killer Mystery (SKM) · Psychological Thriller (PT) · Police Procedural (PP) · Paranormal Mystery (PM) · Occult Mystery (OM) · Noir Mystery (NM) · Legal Thriller (LT) · Historical Mystery (HM) · Heist and Caper Mystery (HCM) · Hard-Boiled Mystery (HBM) · Gothic Mystery (GM) · Forensic Mystery (FM) · Cozy Mystery (CM) · Amateur Sleuth (AS)

Plot Device Tropes (rows).

Plot Device Trope	W	STM	SKM	PT	PP	PM	OM	NM	LT	HM	HCM	HBM	GM	FM	CM	AS
Art										✓	✓				✓	
Betrayal	✓							✓			✓					
Blackmail	✓			✓					✓							
Cat & Mouse				✓	✓							✓				
Cold Case					✓											✓
Conspiracies		✓		✓			✓	✓		✓						
Crime Syndicate					✓			✓	✓							
Cults & Secret Societies		✓		✓		✓	✓						✓			
Kidnapping	✓			✓					✓							
MacGuffin	✓									✓	✓					
Missing Person	✓	✓		✓	✓										✓	✓
Political Intrigue				✓						✓		✓				✓
Race Against Time		✓	✓	✓	✓				✓		✓					
Red Herring	✓			✓	✓					✓					✓	✓
Revenge		✓		✓	✓	✓						✓	✓			
Stolen Identity				✓					✓							
Time Travel						✓	✓			✓						
Twist Ending		✓		✓				✓			✓	✓				
Undercover Investigations					✓				✓							
Unsolved Mysteries		✓		✓	✓										✓	
Unreliable Narrator			✓	✓		✓		✓	✓	✓						
Witness Protection		✓			✓				✓							
Wrongful Conviction/Accusation				✓	✓	✓			✓						✓	✓